Rules Britannia

Rules Britannia

The 101 Essential Questions
of Britishness Answered

by Rohan Candappa

with illustrations by Anthony Cockayne

EBURY
PRESS

1 3 5 7 9 10 8 6 4 2

Published in 2007 by Ebury Press, an imprint of Ebury Publishing

A Random House Group Company

Copyright © Rohan Candappa 2007
Illustrations © Antony Cockayne 2007

Rohan Candappa has asserted his right to be identified as the author of this
Work in accordance with the Copyright, Designs and Patents Act 1988

The Random House Group Limited Reg. No. 954009

Addresses for companies within the Random House Group
can be found at www.randomhouse.co.uk

A CIP catalogue record for this book is available from the British Library

Printed in the UK by CPI Mackays, Chatham, ME5 8TD

ISBN 9780091922955

To buy books by your favourite authors and register for offers visit
www.rbooks.co.uk

p69. Extract originally appeared in *Life in the
UK: A Journey to Citizenship* and used by kind permission

pp.138–9. 'At the Turning of the Tide' by A.C. Grayling originally
appeared in *30: At the Turning of the Tide*, published by the
Commission for Racial Equality, 2007, and used by kind permission

p.176. 'This is What We Find': Words & Music by Ian Dury & Mickie
Gallagher; © Warner/Chappell Music Ltd. All rights administered by
Warner/Chappell Music Ltd, London W6 8BS. Reproduced by permission.

pp.241–2. Harold Pinter's speech 'Art, Truth & Politics' © The Nobel
Foundation, 2006, and used by kind permission.

Dedication

Are you a hedge-fund manager or City trader bonused up to your eyeballs, but with no time to find that extra-special present for a loved one, colleague or client? Then this dedication could be just what you're after. For just £9,999.99 you can have your own dedication inserted in all future reprints of *Rules Britannia: The 101 Essential Questions of Britishness Answered*. It's a truly unique gift that is bound to make the lucky recipient realise just what a special person you truly are. And if you can't think of anyone to buy this dedication for, why not just buy it for yourself?

Why?

Because you're worth it!

For full details contact the author. Your call may be recorded for training purposes.

Acknowledgements

Lack of income is always a great incentive to write. That and the sight of a woman on the Tube reading an official guide to Britishness. I thought someone better put the record straight before she got completely the wrong end of the stick. The other thought that occurred to me was that if you woke up one morning and had no idea who you were, one of the first things to do would be to look in the mirror.

I'd also like to thank my editor Ken Barlow, my agent Simon Trewin, and Miranda West who came up with such a good title for this book that I fully intend to claim it was my idea. In addition I am very grateful to Anthony Cockayne for his beautiful scraperboard illustrations that add to the book immeasurably.

Finally, I'd like to thank Jan and C & T for putting up with me and making everything worthwhile.

Rohan Candappa

INTRODUCTION

So, you want to be British?

Good for you!

But as you no doubt have found, it can be jolly hard trying to fit in. That's where this guide will help. It gives you the answers to the 101 Essential Questions of Britishness. Study it well and you'll soon discover that being British isn't something to worry about, it's something to be enjoyed. And before long you too will be eating cucumber sandwiches, going down the *rub-a-dub* for a swift 'half', and enjoying free speech and the benefits of a first-past-the-post system of representative democracy based on a two-tier set-up of upper and lower houses of legislative power, just like the rest of us.

Rules Britannia

The 101 Essential Questions

~ 1 ~

We British are famous for our Stiff Upper Lip, but in a crisis isn't it the lower one that tends to quiver?

Yes.

What we are dealing with here is an inspired piece of misdirection. Just as a magician will confuse an audience with all manner of flim-flammery to get away with whatever trick he's attempting, so our canny British forebears pointed out how stiff their collective upper lips were when things started to go awry. But they did it with such confidence that no one cottoned on to the truth: namely, they were just as scared as everyone else. The secret was not to let anyone know. Hence the legend of the Stiff Upper Lip was born.

Genius.

~ 2 ~

How do you make a cup of tea?

It's very simple.

First put a tea bag in a teacup. Then boil a kettle of water. Then pour the water into the cup. Next allow the tea to 'brew' for three to five minutes, depending on how strong you like it. Then remove the tea bag and add milk. Sugar can also be added for, naturally enough, sweetness.

Tea can also be made in a teapot. This involves the placing of several tea bags in the pot, adding the water, and letting it brew before tipping it out into individual cups. Traditionalists favour the use of loose tea leaves rather than tea bags, often measuring out the amount of tea to be used with the spoonful-of-tea counting mantra of 'one for each (person) and one for the pot'.

Purists take the whole process even further by refusing to use tap water as the lime content of it can make tea cloudy. They also steer clear of water with too much iron in it which precipitate tannins in the cup. Chlorinated water is likewise forbidden. And they never use water that has been boiled more than once. But that's the thing with purists, they are slightly bonkers. After all just look how much trouble religious purists have made in this world.

Although the making of a cup of tea is a relatively simple and straightforward affair, the meaning of a cup of tea in Britain is anything but simple and straightforward. If a drink can be a crossroads of national identity then a cup of tea is a veritable Spaghetti Junction.

For you, as a newcomer to Britain, how you make a cup of tea is, of course, entirely up to you. What is important, however, is that you do drink tea. Even if you don't actually like the stuff, to be seen drinking a cup of tea is a subtly coded message that speaks of a quiet desire to fit in. Equally important to understand is that when anyone ever comes to visit you it is imperative to offer them a cup of tea. Whether they accept the offer or not is immaterial, what is important is that you make the offer. If the offer is accepted the next request that you should make of your guest is 'how do you take it?' It is through these ritualised steps that the British establish contact with each other.

Of late, coffee and coffee drinking, has seen a sudden surge in popularity. This is a trend that should be resisted. It plays into a mistaken idea of sophistication. This, frankly, pseudo-sophistication has been encouraged by the proliferation of 'continental' coffee shops that offer 'coffee' in a range of options so confusing that it won't be long before 'coffee studies' is taught in schools as a core part of the national curriculum. Tea, by contrast, provides far more accessible pleasures.

In addition, how tea and coffee work psychologically are significantly different. A cup of coffee may well pick you up, but a cup of tea sits you down and has a chat. So tea is fundamentally friendlier than coffee. What's more, tea spans and unites the British social spectrum in a way that coffee never could. At the top end you have, for example, tea at the Ritz. It's all lace doilies, cucumber sandwiches with the crusts cut off, scones with jam and clotted cream, and a surprisingly large bill. At the opposite end it's a bacon sarnie and a mug of tea at a caff for less than a couple of quid. Each experience is as valid, enjoyable, and essentially British as the other.

Indeed so beloved are the subtleties of tea drinking to the British people that they frequently bring them into their own homes. Often when offered a cup of tea at someone's home you will be taxed with the additional question 'cup or mug?' Think about your response carefully as each reply has a different meaning. As a rule it's best to say 'mug' as this speaks of a relaxed informality. And of an artisan willingness to get on with whatever job is in hand.

The power implicit from such a seemingly innocent choice can be gauged from the fact that occasionally our ex-Prime Minister Mr Tony Blair would step out of the door of No. 10 Downing Street to address a press conference with a mug of tea in his hand. Had he come out with a cup of tea it would have sent out a completely different message about his character, his carefully considered image, and how he approached the complex and demanding task of running the country.

On top of all this, tea is the universal lubricant that prevents our great nation from grinding to a halt. In any given situation, we may not know what to do, what to say or how to make real human contact with one another, but we do know how to make a cup of tea. And so that's what we do. Miraculously, that's often all it takes to get things moving.

~ 3 ~

Can you arrange these ten members of the Royal Family in order of height?

1 Prince Philip
2 Prince Charles
3 Princess Anne
4 The Queen Mother
5 Prince Edward
6 Her Majesty the Queen (without crown)
7 Prince Andrew
8 Camilla, Duchess of Cornwall
9 Her Majesty the Queen (with crown)
10 A corgi

Answer

The correct order in ascending height is The Queen Mother, Her Majesty The Queen (without crown), Princess Anne, Her Majesty The Queen (with crown), Camilla Duchess of Cornwall, Prince Charles, Prince Philip, Prince Edward, Prince Andrew. As for the corgi, whilst it may be regarded as a member of the Royal Household it is not, officially, a member of the Royal Family. However no one has ever been brave enough to actually explain this to the corgis.

~ 4 ~

Where should I join a queue?

Nothing is more British than queuing. Indeed, if queuing ever became an Olympic sport Britain would undoubtedly win gold every time. Or we would until we taught the other nations the rules for queuing and then, much to our horror, we would discover that the foreigners had learned to do it better. (But this too is a grand British tradition.)

Mind you, the rules aren't hard to learn. In its most basic form queuing involves standing in a first come, first served line in order to achieve some specific goal.

What could be simpler?

The very existence of the habit and practice of queuing speaks of a nation that is at ease with itself and in which order, harmony, and justice prevail. And that is the key aspect of queuing. Queuing is all about fairness. And fairness is a concept very dear to the heart, lungs, liver and kidneys of every Briton.

If you are a novice queuer and nervous about joining in this national pastime then just follow these simple instructions and before long you too will be queuing like a native. When you turn up at a place where a queue has formed, join the back of the queue and patiently wait your turn to get to the front. The back of the queue will be easy to spot as it will be the end where you are confronted by the back of a fellow queuer. If you join the queue and are confronted by another person's face then you have inadvertently joined the front of the queue. This practice is deeply frowned upon. Your best bet is to make your apologies and make haste to the other end of the queue.

Equally unacceptable is joining the middle of the queue. Even tactics such as chatting to a friend you have spied halfway down the queue will draw looks of disapproval. This is because, happy though the people in the queue will no doubt be that you have a friend in the queue, queue etiquette outweighs the bonds of friendship.

Indeed, so deeply ingrained are the rules of queuing in the British psyche that in 1946 George Mikes was given to remark in his best-selling book *How To Be An Alien* that 'An Englishman, even if he is alone, forms an orderly queue of one'.

What is just as British, but probably more revealing, about the British love of queuing, is the assumption that those from other shores don't know how to queue. This is a state of mind that assumes a breathtaking degree of cultural and intellectual superiority. As such it is an undoubted throwback to the days of the British Empire when an assumption of cultural and intellectual superiority was as deeply ingrained as any windswept resort's name in a tooth-rotting stick of seaside rock.

Unfortunately, as the Empire dissolved, broke up and generally legged it for the exits, maintaining the belief in Britain's cultural and intellectual pre-eminence proved harder to sustain. And when those ungrateful bastards started to regularly trounce the Mother Country at cricket it all became too much to take.

So surely there was one achievement this once great nation could cling to for comfort? Thankfully, there was. And it was the concept and practice of queuing. That almost wherever you go in the world queues can be found was conveniently forgotten. Britain steadfastly holds to the belief that like the steam engine, the industrial revolution, the computer and Celebrity Big Brother, we gave queuing to the world.

All of which explains why, if you are a newcomer to these shores, one of the best ways to fit in is to join in the national pastime of queuing for things. Indeed the only better way to blend in than queuing for things is to adopt the right attitude towards people who don't queue for things. The right attitude being – depending on circumstances – disappointment, distaste, disapproval or suppressed rage.

And to be truly at one with the British psyche, under extreme queue etiquette breakdown you might even try sliding out of the corner of a tensely clamped mouth the barely audible tirade '...there is a queue you know'.

~ 5 ~

Does 'political correctness' ever get mildly annoyed?

No, 'political correctness' never gets mildly annoyed, it only ever 'goes mad'. This is an inevitable consequence of the fact that there is no 'political correctness' continuum.

'Political correctness' exists and then 'political correctness gone mad' exists. Between these two states of being you will not find political correctness being slightly troubled, political correctness being uneasy, political correctness being mildly annoyed, political correctness being concerned, political correctness being not happy, political correctness being put out, political correctness being peeved, political correctness having got out of the wrong side of the bed in the morning, political correctness having a cob on, political correctness being pissed off, political correctness being well-pissed off, or indeed, political correctness spitting feathers.

There is either 'political correctness', or there is 'political correctness gone mad'. There is nothing in between.

In this way political correctness is very like carbon, which is either a lump of coal, or a diamond.

~ 6 ~

*If you were standing at a bus stop
and nothing happened for ages
how many buses should you expect
to turn up all at once?*

One bus would be the sensible answer. Two buses would
be mildly annoying. Three buses would really piss you off.

For this reason you should expect three buses.

However, statistically speaking, this is in fact the least
likely turn of events. But it is the one that looms largest
in the collective consciousness of the British traveller.
Contrary to popular belief, this isn't an example of
national pessimism. After all if the British were a
pessimistic people then we would expect to wait ages at a
bus stop and have no bus turn up. Ever.

If we waited ages at a bus stop and then expected two
buses to turn up at the same time, we would be a people
who are used to a certain amount of incompetence in our
daily dealings with the modern world.

But we, as a people, wait ages at a bus stop, then
expect *three* buses to turn up. What this taps into is a fear
of collusion amongst those with petty degrees of power
over us. After all, three buses couldn't turn up at once

A bus stop

unless the drivers of the three buses were working on the basis of some kind of tacit agreement. It may well be that the agreement had been worked out explicitly before-hand, but what the British really dread is that the agreement was, in fact, unspoken. What this feeds on is the underlying fear that we are all somehow in the power of forces, conventions and, ultimately, groups of people over which we have no influence.

In other countries such a concern might manifest itself as a fear of the power of politicians, or the functionings of the capitalist system. But in Britain it is the distrust of those with petty amounts of power over us that most defines our paranoia. Hence 'Disgusted of Tunbridge Wells' does not get exercised by the failings and foibles of Britain's market-driven capitalist economy, but rather by the fact the local council have painted a yellow line on the road outside the newsagent's where he parks each morning in order to buy his copy of the *Daily Telegraph*.

So, in conclusion, wait ages at a bus stop and while the chances are it is one bus that will turn up, expect three. Do that and you will be one step closer to being truly British.

~ 7 ~

Which comedy catchphrases should I know?

A catchphrase is a curious thing. In essence it is a collection of often-repeated words that provides for the listener a moment of recognition and comfort. Indeed, hear a catchphrase and you, figuratively speaking, know where you are in the world. All of which makes the catchphrase the verbal equivalent of one of those massive black arrows you see on publicly displayed maps along with the profoundly reassuring information 'YOU ARE HERE'. After all, if you are, indeed, 'HERE' then you can't be anywhere else, and you most definitely can't be lost.

For the person uttering the catchphrase the words work in much the same way. They both define and confirm who they are. The downside of this state of affairs is that should the catchphrase prove to be too successful, the catchphraser runs the risk of being solely defined in the mind of the catchphrasee by the words of the catchphrase. In fact the damned thing can often follow them round like a particularly dedicated stalker hell-bent on wrecking their subsequent careers.

Everywhere the cathchphraser goes the catchphrase is

thrown at them by a public who expect their victim to smile benignly when really, deep down inside, their very being is screaming 'Noooooooouuoooooooooooooooooooo-o!'

And that, in a nutshell, is the kernel of the conundrum that is the catchphrase. It starts off defining who someone is, but, if truly successful, ends up denying who someone is.

For anyone aspiring to be British, however, all this philosophical musing is of secondary importance to being au fait with the catchphrases that have lodged themselves in the collective consciousness of the nation. Below are listed the key comedic catchphrases of the last sixty years.

1   'He's fallen in the water' – the words of Little Jim in the 1950s radio programme *The Goon Show*. Of particular use should you ever encounter His Royal Highness Prince Charles at a bus stop and have to engage him in idle chit-chat.

2   'Hello, my name's Julian and this is my friend Sandy' – originally uttered on the radio show *Round The Horne* by Hugh Paddick. Paddick played Julian and Kenneth Williams played Sandy. What then followed was a comedic sketch in which certain practices were alluded to by the actors, and guffawed at by an audience that enjoyed the frisson

of being 'in the know'. (NB: fuller explanations of the phrase are available at al fresco evening classes after dark on Hampstead Heath).

3 'You dirty old man' – Harold Steptoe's perennial line to his father Albert in the TV show *Steptoe and Son*. It is a phrase that resonates with a 1970s attitude to sex and sexuality that only allowed the repressed British male to deal with the subject by recourse to, and here comes another key 1970s concept, smut.

4 'Don't panic!' 'We're doomed ...' 'Stupid boy' – A selection of catchphrases from the sitcom *Dad's Army*. For many reasons, in any consideration of what makes the British British, *Dad's Army* probably deserves a whole book to itself. It combined in every thirty-minute episode war nostalgia, class conflict and self-deprecation. But shot right through the gags and pratfalls is a fierce, if somewhat reticent, national pride. That the idealised Britain represented by Warmington-on-Sea has long since disappeared is a loss that many people still mourn. And that Private Pike now looks old enough to be cast in Clive Dunn's role, but instead plies his trade on *EastEnders*, is a sadness too great to contemplate.

5 'This is an ex-parrot' – a catchphrase from the vastly overrated *Monty Python's Flying Circus*. It appears in a sketch in which a man buys a parrot that subsequently turns out to have been dead all along. If you can't see why this is funny, or, indeed, important to the furtherment of civilisation in the latter part of the twentieth century, don't worry. Just turn on your TV late at night and sooner or later you're bound to encounter a seventeen-part documentary series explaining it all to you. Probably presented by Jimmy Carr.

6 'You plonker, Rodney' – A criticism made by the unfailingly failing 1980s wheeler-dealer Del Boy Trotter of his younger brother Rodney in the Peckham-based sitcom *Only Fools And Horses*. It was a series that chimed with the times by crashing the get-rich-quick aspirations of the Thatcherite boom years into the harsh realities of those with limited resources, opportunities and skills. The key lesson to be learned from the series in terms of understanding Britishness is that Del Boy never makes it. He always screws it up. He always fails. And yet the nation loves him. As such the whole ethos of the show, and indeed a whole strand of Britishness is summed up in the word 'plonker'. It is a term of rebuke. But it's also a term of affection.

7 'I don't believe it' – The words of wisdom oft repeated by Victor Meldrew in the series *One Foot In The Grave*. A succinct and pointed summation of the point of view of that most British of characters: Disgusted Of Tunbridge Wells. A character who, when you're young, you think is a ludicrous has-been. But, as you get older, starts to talk a lot of sense.

8 'Am I bovvered?' – The era-defining catchphrase of Catherine Tate's character Lauren. Three words that both criticise and celebrate the incomprehensibly graffitied wall of the dead-end that is Yoof Kulcha. Innit.

This is not to say that these catchphrases are the most important words ever written in the English language. Rather, if you do know them, and what they represent, you're several canned studio laughs closer to being a part of it all.

Or, to misquote a catchphrase from another essentially British comedy show, 'They're local jokes, for local people…'

~ 8 ~

Which political sound bites should I know?

A political sound bite is a curious thing. In essence it is a collection of often-repeated words that provide for the listener a moment of recognition and comfort. Indeed, hear a political sound bite and you, figuratively speaking, know where you are in the world. All of which makes the political sound bite the verbal equivalent of one of those massive black arrows you see on publicly displayed maps along with the profoundly reassuring information, 'YOU ARE HERE'. After all, if you are, indeed 'HERE' then you can't be anywhere else, and you most definitely can't be lost.

For the person uttering the political sound bite the words work in much the same way. They both define and confirm who they are. The downside of this state of affairs is that should the political sound bite prove to be too successful, the sound biter runs the risk of being solely defined in the mind of the sound bitten by the words of the sound bite. In fact the damned thing can often follow them round like a particularly dedicated stalker hell-bent on wrecking their subsequent careers.

Everywhere the sound biter goes the sound bite is thrown at them by a public who expect their victim to smile benignly when really, deep down inside, their very being is screaming 'Nooooooooooooooooooooooooooooo -o!'

And that, in a nutshell, is the kernel of the conundrum that is the political sound bite. It starts off defining who someone is, but, if truly successful, ends up denying who someone is.

The most interesting political sound bite uttered in recent years was used by David Cameron on being elected leader of the Conservative party. It was aimed at the ageing Tony Blair. It was:

'You were the future once.'

What is particularly commendable about Mr Cameron's choice of these five simple words is that not only did they mark the arrival of a formidable new force in British politics, but they will also inevitably provide the epitaph for that selfsame force's eventual failure.

So far-sighted a politician is most definitely one to watch.

~ 9 ~

Which sport did the British invent and can still beat the world at?

Conkers.

~ 10 ~

Is it better to pickle a conker in vinegar or to bake it in the oven?

A conker is the seed of the horse chestnut tree. This hard brown nut develops in a spiky green case that falls to the ground in the autumn. Then the outer casing is pulled off and the conker extracted.

To play conkers you need two contestants – ideally small- to medium-sized boys – who each have a conker in which a hole has been drilled and a short length of string threaded.

The first player holds his string up in front of him at head height so that the conker hangs, like a pendulum, below. The second player then takes aim with his conker and tries to hit it. If he succeeds in hitting it then the roles are reversed. If he misses he can have up to two more attempts (though rules vary on this point). If the strings get entangled he shouts 'strings' and gets another shot. If the target conker gets knocked to the ground, then as long as the aggressor shouts 'Stamps!' quickly enough, he can stamp on his opponent's conker and crush it. However, if the player whose conker has been knocked to the ground shouts 'No stamps!' before the other player has shouted 'Stamps!' then the fallen conker cannot, legally, be crushed under foot.

Obviously, these circumstances can lead to 'who shouted what first' disputes. Traditionally these incidents are settled by a short 'bundle' or fight between the two aggrieved parties. Accusations of 'cheat!' are often hurled at these moments. Then the two factions separate and go home for their tea, threatening never to play with each other again. However, by the next day, things are usually back on an even keel.

Scoring is recorded by how many conkers the winning conker has destroyed. A conker that has won one fight is called a 'one-er', a conker that has won two fights is called a 'two-er'. However if a conker destroys a conker that itself has already won a number of fights then it adds its enemies tally to its own score. For example if a 'two-er' defeated a 'four-er' then it would become a 'six-er'. As can be seen from this system of scoring, fame and glory in the world of conkers can be rapidly accrued. All you have to do is beat the champion. In this respect conkers is very like boxing.

The other key ritual aspect of conkers is the gathering of them. Obviously the easiest way to do this is to collect the conkers from the ground when they fall. However, this is ultimately an unsatisfactory approach as there is no skill in picking things up from the ground. Just as the gladiators of ancient Rome had to win their way through preliminary battles to earn the right to fight in the Coliseum, so the really prized conker is the one that has to be knocked off the highest branch by a well-aimed stick hurled by a small boy who knows he's going to get chased away if the park keeper spots him. Unfortunately, this is a tradition that is, in an age of PlayStations, Game Boys and computers in children's bedrooms, fast disappearing from the nation. Perhaps what is needed to revive the tradition is to adapt it to the modern world. And surely it can't be mere coincidence that an old mobile phone is nigh on the perfect size and weight to hurl at a tree?

As for the question that started this section, it refers to the ways in which conker aficionados attempt to improve the durability and toughness of their conkers. Baking in an oven, pickling in vinegar, or indeed putting a conker away at the back of a sock drawer for a year, are all traditional ways of creating a potential champion conker. However, the latest scientific research into the subject revealed a rather surprising alternative. It showed that the most effective way of toughening up a conker was to rub it with hand cream. The cream, apparently, softened the conker so that when it was struck by another the impact was dissipated.

This shocking revelation has wide-ranging implications for the world of conkers. It may also have intriguing implications for how hand creams are advertised on TV. And surely it can only be a matter of time before Laboratoire Garnier and Procter & Gamble start slugging it out with big-money deals to sponsor the World Conker Championships.

~ 11 ~

You have an unspecified number of eggs, but only one basket. How many of the eggs should you keep in that basket?

Not all of them.

The problem being that if you were to keep all the eggs in one basket, and then dropped that basket, there's a very real chance the eggs would break. While this may seem an unduly pessimistic view of your basket-carrying abilities it is an approach that, in Britain, is taken to be common sense.

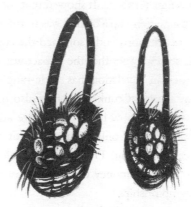

A solution

The obvious solution would be to have two baskets. But, let's be frank, if you can't be trusted to carry one basket without dropping it would adding another basket to what you're laden with really be such a good idea?

It is also worth noting that the standard advice to not 'put all your eggs in one basket' ignores the fact that if you are involved in an eggs-in-basket scenario in the first place you must, presumably, be intending to go somewhere with the eggs. Given this state of affairs, even if you don't 'put all your eggs in one basket', what are you supposed to do with the other eggs? Maybe you're just meant to leave them on the ground, then make an initial trip with the eggs in your basket, unload these eggs at your destination, then return to the eggs you had left behind and load them into the basket to make a second trip. But, as I'm sure you have realised by now, this approach is also fraught with many potential egg hazards.

Another point worth considering is that no standard advice exists on what to do in the far more frequently occurring state of affairs of having only one egg, but a choice of baskets in which to store it.

Given all this, perhaps the best solution is to steer clear of eggs altogether.

~ 12 ~

Who or what is really there in a 'knock-knock' joke?

The format of a knock-knock joke is simplicity itself. It is, in essence, a charade played out between two people.

The protagonist, or knocker, verbally pretends to knock on an imaginary door. The antagonist, or knockee, verbally tries to ascertain who it is that is knocking on the imaginary door and trying to gain entry to an equally imaginary interior whose precise nature is never explicitly described.

The exchange proceeds through a dialogue the specific nature of which may change, but the form of which does not.

The joke ends with the knocker resolving the knockee's query with a verbal riposte that usually involves a pun or a play on words.

For example:

Knocker:	Knock-knock!
Knockee:	Who's there?
Knocker:	Cowsgo.
Knockee:	Cowsgo who?
Knocker:	No they don't, they go mooo!

Or:

Knocker:	Knock-knock!
Knockee:	Who's there?
Knocker:	Isabel.
Knockee:	Isabel who?
Knocker:	Isabel necessary on a bicycle?

As can be seen from these examples a successful knock-knock joke doesn't have to be that funny. All a successful knock-knock joke has to do is conform to the format.

Hence if someone with whom you are innocently conversing about the price of fish suddenly, apropos of absolutely nothing, says 'knock-knock', just remember to say 'who's there?' as opposed to the far more logical 'what?' Then continue the exchange through its ritualised stages which, by convention, should end with you giving a mock pained expression and a small groan.

Whatever you do, don't end the exchange with uproarious laughter. No one expects anyone to laugh at a knock-knock joke. Laugh at a knock-knock joke and you will be suspected of 'having a laugh' and may well end up being thumped.

However, if it is a small child who is the knocker, then you, the knockee, should laugh.

Ideally, having been on the receiving end of a knock-knock joke you should be able to instigate one yourself. Once again how funny the joke is doesn't really matter.

It is the fact you understand the form that is the key. It is also worth noting that only one joke is required. Attempting more is extremely ill-advised.

Interestingly, some scholars have traced the origin of the knock-knock joke to the greatest Briton who ever lived – William Shakespeare. Act 2 Scene III of the Bard's play *Macbeth* (or *The Scottish Play* if you're reading this in a theatre) contains the following lines:

> *Porter:*   Knock, knock!
>   Who's there, i th'name of Beelzebub?
>   Here's a farmer that hang'd
>   Himself on th'expectation of plenty.

Which only goes to show that whilst Shakespeare may well have been the master of sonnets and a genius of a playwright, he never really got the hang of knock-knock jokes.

Other researches have revealed that the origin of the knock-knock joke may have been far earlier. The following is an exchange tracked down in a pre-publication, uncorrected proof copy of the King James Bible. The dialogue was left out of subsequent versions of The Book Of Genesis as it cast a somewhat controversial theological light on the reasons for man's banishment from the Garden of Eden.

And then Eve spaketh saying 'Knock-knock'
And Adam replyeth unto her saying 'Who's there ?'

And Eve spaketh once more saying 'Eve'
And Adam sayeth 'Eve who?'
And Eve's countenance was sore troubled at the
    obtutheneth of Adam as she spaketh
'Eve' n you should know I'm the only other
    person here –
Now where's that Granny Smiths I waseth saving
    for my tea?'
And Adam sayeth 'Oops...'

Just as knock-knock jokes go back to the earliest days of
man, they are also a format that can be easily updated to
accommodate an ever-changing zeitgeist. At the time of
writing the following is the very latest knock-knock joke.

'Knock-knock'
'Who's there?'
'Doctor.'
'Doctor who?'
'Doctor *whom*!'
'You're Lynne Truss, aren't you...'

However, by far the greatest English language exponent of
the knock-knock joke was the playwright Samuel Beckett.
Indeed, consider almost any work from his extensive
oeuvre and it can ultimately be resolved into an exploration of the set-up of the classic knock-knock joke as:

Voice One: Knock-knock.
Voice Two: Who's there?

All of which brings us rather neatly to the query originally posed. Who or what is really there in a knock-knock joke?

Work back from Beckett's position and the answer is clear. No one is there. Yet we are there. And we are nothing more, but nothing less, than imaginary characters, mouthing ritualised nonsensical queries, that we hope will enable an imaginary door to be opened, that will gain us access to an equally imaginary interior, but in reality it matters not one jot if the door is opened, as all that is important is that we complete the steps of the ritual and arrive at the conclusion of what is supposedly a joke, but a joke that everyone understands does not have to be funny.

Clearly the knock-knock joke is telling us that life is meaningless, but paradoxically it is the very meaningless of life that gives it its meaning.

Concur with this analysis and it becomes obvious that who or what is really there in a knock-knock joke is a revelation of the ultimate truth of our very existence. A truth best summed up in the following, profound, exchange.

'Knock-knock!'
'Who's there?'
'Boo.'

'Boo who?'
'Don't cry, it's only a joke'.

~ 13 ~

In Britain how many management consultants does it take to change a light bulb?

It all depends on whether it's a publicly funded project.

~ 14 ~

What is rebranding?

Rebranding is the process by which something tries to change its image, its perception and, ultimately, its reality, by changing its name. Obviously this goes against the view William Shakespeare put forward when he sonnetly remarked '*A rose by any other name would smell as sweet*'. Perhaps this may well have been the case back in the 1600s when the Bard of Avon was barding in Avon, but these days any number of 'brand consultants' would make a good fist of arguing the contrary. After all, as the consultants would no doubt have put it:

> 'Yes, William we can see your point, on one level, if we called a rose, for instance a roose, of course it would still smell as sweet, but what if we called it a *new* rose – wouldn't it somehow imply to the potential rose consumer demographic an entirely enhanced rose experience?'

Obviously the easiest time for anything to be rebranded is if the thing in question has actually changed. Change, however, is often hard to effect. Which is why the British public has an inbuilt scepticism about rebranding. What concerns us is that rebrandings are often nothing more than sleight of hand exercises designed to disguise what, in reality, is a lack of change. This suspicion is heightened by the fact that rebrandings most frequently happen to things with a negative image. Hence British Steel became Corus. The Post Office became Consignia. And Windscale, the nuclear reactor that was the site of a leak of radioactive iodine-131 back in 1957, became Sellafield twenty-four years later.

That the people who ran the power station should think it worthwhile changing its name so long after the leak is interesting. Especially as the iodine released had a half-life of only eight days. Unfortunately the negative image the incident created lingered in the complex food chain of the national memory far more persistently.

Perhaps the most successful rebranding of recent times has been in the field of politics. When Tony Blair took control of his party he changed its name from Labour to New Labour. On the face of it, it was a crass, almost ludicrously simplistic move. But it worked. And it worked for one very simple reason. That simple reason being that people *wanted* a new Labour party. How new the New Labour party actually was before it got elected as the New Labour party is open to debate.

Sometimes rebranding happens for other reasons. For example, Marathon chocolate bars became Snickers, and

Jif bathroom cleaner became Cif, for reasons of 'global rationalisation'. What this really means is that it saves money for the multinational companies producing them. So, bizarrely, these were two examples of rebranding where the rebranders were desperate to point out what had been rebranded was exactly the same as it was before. Only with a different name.

But these are exceptions. More often than not rebranding is about changing perceptions. For example, why else would 'unemployment benefit' become 'job-seekers allowance'?

Of particular interest to you as a newcomer to Britain is the fact that, should you wish, you could rebrand yourself. All you have to do is to change your name. In the past this was done so that people who had recently, or even not so recently, settled in the country would find themselves more easily accepted.

For instance, back in the 1950s Vasily Petrovich Mironov found himself in Ilford in Essex. At the time Vasilys were quite thin on the ground in the county. So he started calling himself Basil and anglicised the obviously Russian surname. His young daughter, Ilyena, also had to change her name. She became Helen Mirren.

Or take the Yorkshire-born actor of Indian descent, Krishna Bhanji. When he told his father he wanted to be an actor, his father advised him to change his name. To anglicise it. So Krishna Bjanki became Ben Kingsley. And his career took off. He even won an Academy

Award for best actor in a leading role. Ironically, he was playing Gandhi.

So, in order to make his name, he had changed it from an Indian one. But then he actually made his name by playing a man with the most Indian of Indian names. All of which raises the intriguing question as to what would have happened if he'd been working under his original name of Krishna Bhanji when he played Gandhi? Would he have won the Oscar?

However the most significant example of personal rebranding in Britain occurred at the very top of the social system. In 1917, three years into a largely pointless World War that destroyed millions of lives, anti-German sentiment was at its height. Consequently, having a German-sounding name in Britain wasn't a very good idea. This presented a somewhat tricky situation for the King, George the Fifth, as his family name was Saxe-Coburg-Gotha. But with a little judicious rebranding, and the renouncing of his German titles, he renamed the royal family the House of Windsor. He chose Windsor as it was the name of the castle where he resided. All of which kind of makes you wish he'd been living in nearby Slough.

~ 15 ~

*How many recipes should Britons use
from the latest celebrity chef cookbook
that they get given at Christmas?*

Three.

But, in reality, they need only regularly return to two of those three recipes. The other recipes in the book are primarily included to be leafed through, whilst cooing over the unbelievably scrumptious-looking photographs, but then ignored as being too complicated, too time-consuming, or requiring the purchase of ingredients that will only be used for that particular recipe and hence will end up at the back of a kitchen cupboard until you move house.

In this regard celebrity chef cookbooks are much like Colman's mustard who, it was once said, made their profits by what gets left on the side of the plate.

~ 16 ~

What amazing power does the 'wrong kind of snow' have?

The 'wrong kind of snow' has the power to stop trains.

As a newcomer to this country you may well be visualising the problem as being one of six-foot deep drifts of sparkling white snow burying tracks so completely that nothing can pass. This would be an understandable error to make. However, as the question states, what we're dealing with here is not the wrong *amount* of snow, but the wrong *kind* of snow. It's a problem of quality, not quantity.

All of which begs the question what kind of snow, precisely, are we talking about?

Even the Eskimos, who supposedly have forty-nine different words for different types of snow, don't have one for snow that has the power to stop trains. Mind you, trains aren't big in the Arctic, so maybe the issue has never arisen.

The phrase 'the wrong kind of snow', which is actually a misquote, came to prominence in February 1991 when the Director of Operations for British Rail was asked to explain why there had been so many train delays and cancellations when BR had known a 'cold snap' was on the way. His actual answer was, 'We are having particular problems with the type of snow'.

The snow that was causing the problems was unusually fine, soft and powdery. It was getting into the electrical systems causing short circuits and traction motor damage. But this was too detailed an explanation. Instead the media seized on the seemingly ridiculous excuse that the trains had been cancelled due to the 'wrong type of snow'.

The absurdity of it struck a chord with the British public. After all, how could something as big and powerful as a train be stopped by something as fragile and ephemeral as snow? But the main reason the excuse found a home in the collective British consciousness is that it seemed to crystallise the malaise that had gripped the national railway system for so long. British Rail was so pathetic that the slightest bit of snow and the whole thing ground to a halt. Subsequently all that arrived on time was a ridiculous excuse.

What this all plays into is the deep-seated fear amongst a large proportion of the British populous that we aren't very good at anything. Especially running the country. And its infrastructure. To understand why the manifestation of this fear, in connection with anything to do with the railways, should be so powerful a metaphor for the state of the nation as a whole you have to understand the prominent place the railways occupies in the subconscious of the country.

Britain invented the railways. Stephenson's *Rocket* changed the world. And with the steam engine and the railways came the Industrial Revolution. What's more, the Age of Steam was the one in which Britain came to dominate vast parts of the globe. Hence the railways were a symbol of Britain's power and success.

On top of all this the railways hold a special place in the nation's cultural imagination. There's *Thomas The Tank Engine*. There's *The Railway Children*. There's *Brief Encounter*. There's Auden's poem *The Night Mail*. There's *The Great Train Robbery*. There's even platform 9¾ at King's Cross from which Harry Potter catches the train to get to Hogwarts.

A train

In short the railways mean much more in Britain than a way of getting from A to B. So any difficulty with the railways resonates far more in the heart of every Briton than a comparable problem on, for example, the M4.

Which brings us back to the original question.

What amazing power does the 'wrong kind of snow' have?

It has the power to make a once great nation wonder where it all went wrong. But as this is still, albeit in different ways, a great nation, we ponder the question with a light dusting of wryness. Whether it's the 'wrong kind of wryness' is another question entirely.

~ 17 ~

What cockney rhyming slang should I know?

This is a trick question. Knowledge of cockney rhyming slang for a newcomer is always suspect. Nothing will mark you out more quickly as someone who has only recently arrived in the country than 'casually' dropping into the conversation that you're off down the 'frog and toad' (road) to visit the 'rub-a-dub' (pub). It would be like a dad trying to 'get down' with his kids by wearing a hoodie, greeting them ' Yo Bredr'n, wassuppp!' then taking his leave by exclaiming 'Laters!' while attempting to do a 'hoo-ha' with his 'frims'.

Perhaps the worst example of this embarrassing behaviour occurred when, after moving to England, Madonna started the first London concert of her Apples 'N' Pears Tour by appearing as a scantily clad pearly queen doing a decidedly raunchy cockney style knees-up on a rooftop and chimney Mary Poppins-esque set, while lip-synching the rhyming slangily rewritten lyrics to the three opening numbers. 'Like A Virgin' became 'Pike A Sturgeon'. 'Vogue' became 'Minogue'. And 'La Isla Bonita' became 'I Eata Ryvita'.

It was after this debacle that the shadowy and secretive Cockney Council of senior cabbies, costermongers and ex-ILEA dinner ladies met and voted unanimously to move the diverse, often warring, yet somehow unified tribes of the Cockney Nation away from rhyming slang. In its place they instigated a whole new language. It is a language that, until now, has remained a closely guarded secret. Below are reproduced, for the very first time, a handful of words from that new language. Cockney Unrhyming Slang:

Oranges & lemons – escalator
Bacardi Breezer – cashpoint
Norman Lamont – futon
Chutney – mini cash ISA
Steak & kidney pie – laptop

~ 18 ~

Liz Hurley. Explain.

Liz Hurley is a woman best known for wearing a dress.

She is also an actress who has appeared in Hollywood smashes, an international spokesmodel for a multi-million pound cosmetics brand, the wronged girlfriend of a disgraced movie superstar, a single mother who had to prove the paternity of her child to her millionaire ex-boyfriend, and the blushing bride in what may well have been the longest wedding in history.

Yet she is still best known for wearing a dress.

The dress in question was one designed by Gianni Versace that, despite costing hundreds of pounds, was 'wittily' held together by designer safety pins. Liz wore the dress one night in 1994 when she went to the pictures with her then boyfriend.

The picture they were going to see was the premiere of *Four Weddings And A Funeral*, and her then boyfriend was the leading man of the movie, Hugh Grant. The film turned Grant into a superstar. The dress turned Hurley into something far rarer.

She became a person who was famous just for being famous. She became a celebrity whose celebrity was based on nothing more than being a celebrity. And while it was based on nothing more than that, it was also based on nothing less than that. Which is a subtle, but important, point and goes some way to explaining why Liz Hurley is a true icon of the Britain in which we live.

Much to Liz's credit, she knows that celebrity is a ravenous beast that needs constant feeding. Fail to provide a steady diet of juicy morsels and there's every chance that the creature will turn and devour you whole.

Over the years Liz has tipped into the feeding trough of the ever-hungry creature a succession of relationships, a series of minor movie roles, an abortive movie production company, a switch into TV presenting, a decade-long stint as the face of Estée Lauder, a launch of Liz Hurley Beach: 'an international luxury lifestyle brand', a week-long wedding, and, in what is probably the true signifier of her marketing genius, a prime-time, nationally networked interview with the American talk-show host Barbara Walters in which she 'shared her pain' at her partner, Hugh Grant, being caught in a car, in Hollywood, with a prostitute called Divine Brown.

In a 2002 interview she even referred to non-celebrities as 'civilians'. She then went on to say that she could never marry a 'civilian' as they wouldn't be able 'to handle the pressure'. At another time she remarked, 'Being thin is my job. I go to bed hungry.'

All of which is a decidedly warped view of the world. But then again if, just by wearing a designer dress held together by safety pins, you find yourself in a decidedly warped world, then realigning how you view things may be the only way to survive. Or, indeed, prosper.

All of which makes Liz Hurley a latter-day version of that other oh-so-British heroine Alice, who fell down a rabbit hole and found herself in an absurd Land of Wonders.

It's just that this particular Alice decided that she rather likes it down the rabbit hole. And, consequently, has tried to make the most of it.

~ 19 ~

What are the four most important British fish beginning with the letter H?

Herring.
Haddock.
Halibut.
Hake.

~ 20 ~

How many store loyalty cards can you possess before you are actually guilty of disloyalty?

The truth is that in Britain today there is no hard and fast rule on this matter. So by resorting to common sense to analyse the problem the obvious conclusion is that it is perfectly acceptable to have one store loyalty card for each kind of store that you frequent.

Therefore you can have a card from one supermarket, a card from one clothes shop, a card from one coffee shop, and a card from one traffic-light windscreen washer.

Should you ever sign up for a card from a category of retailer for which you already possess a competing card, you will find yourself in a most awkward moral and philosophical dilemma. It is a dilemma recognised millennia ago by Jesus himself when confronted by the competing claims on the good people of the Holy Land presented by the expectations of the Roman Empire and the expectations of their religion. His solution was the well-judged judgement:

'Render unto Caesar the things which are
Caesar's, and unto God the things that are God's'

Obviously this will only work if there is a clear distinction
as to what belongs to whom. Rephrase the son of God's
advice in the terms of the dilemma we are currently
considering and the limitations of that advice soon
become apparent:

'Render unto Tesco the things which are Tesco's,
and unto Sainsbury's the things that are
Sainsbury's'

So the only simple solution is to have one loyalty card,
from each type of store.

Unfortunately even this does not prevent the British
store-card holder from facing some very Gordian Knotty
challenges.

The problem lies in the fact that some of Britain's
larger retail emporia are increasingly widening the scope
of goods they offer. Tesco, for example, used to be somewhere you went to shop for food. Now it has whole aisles
devoted to electrical goods, clothing, books, CDs and
the like. It has even branched into intangible products
like insurance. And surely it's only a matter of time
before Tesco sees that there's money to be made by
offering reasonably priced, good-quality plastic surgery,
religion or representative democracy.

As retailers extend their remit then loyalty to one inevitably conflicts with loyalty to others.

Another facet of the loyalty card conundrum that aspirant Britons would do well to consider is what, precisely, does your 'loyalty' imply? For instance, should Britain be invaded by outside forces threatening to lay waste to all we hold dear, will Sir Terry Leahy – chairman of Tesco – find his face plastered over countless posters informing us that 'Your Supermarket Needs You'?

And if that did occur would Sir Philip Hampton – chairman of Sainsbury's – make haste to Broadcasting House and transmit to the nation, in a gruff voice choked with emotion, that your primary loyalty is, in fact, to Sainsbury's, and then raise your patriotic fervour by demanding you join with him on the front line of the produce aisle to confront the foe where '...We'll fight them with the peaches...'?

Obviously this whole interpretation of the concept of 'loyalty' may be a slight misreading of the way British retail endeavours use the term. That's because a more accurate description of how the retailers envisage the cards would be Extremely Valuable Consumer Shopping Habit Monitoring And Data Capture Devices. This, however, is not a particularly appealing name. 'Loyalty Card' works much better.

Incidentally, by far the best card to sign up for at the moment is the IKEA Family Card. Join this scheme and you 'become part of the IKEA family'. The stated benefits are free tea, or coffee, every time you visit and extra discounts on items they've probably over-produced and are desperately trying to get rid off.

However, if by signing up for an IKEA Family Card you do, in fact, 'become part of the IKEA family', then surely, when old man IKEA pops his clogs you'll be in line to inherit a part of the estate. Probably only a small part, as there will be countless others who are also 'part of the IKEA family'. But as the whole business world-wide turns over in excess of 12 billion euros a year it would be well worth while digging out your black tie for the will reading.

~ 21 ~

Can the true nature of the intricacies of the British class system be summed up in the difference between the Argos catalogue and the Lakeland catalogue?

Yes.

~ 22 ~

What should I do if the man next to me starts humming 'The Dam Busters March'?

In many ways the national anthem is the most important tune in Britain.

It is the tune that is played at the start of international sporting events. It is the tune that's played whenever the Queen turns up anywhere. (God, she must be getting bored of it by now. In fact she's probably the only person on the planet who likes to hear a bit of muzak when she gets into a lift). And it is the tune that even used to be played in cinemas before a film started.

However its very ubiquity, while making it undoubtedly universally accepted as nationalistically important, has done little to make it loved. Or even liked.

Very few people would start to hum the national anthem to themselves for a bit of fun.

The tune to the film *The Dam Busters*, however, is a completely different kettle of fish. Humming 'The Dam Busters March' and also doing the approved accompanying actions is uniquely British. And uniquely loved.

The film, made in 1954, tells the story of a heroic

A gnibmob nur

bombing raid made during the Second World War on the Mohne dams in the Ruhr Valley in Germany. The logic behind the raid was that, by destroying the dams, water would be released that would then flood the heavy industrial factories so vital to the German war effort.

It is a stirring tale that speaks volumes about both the bravery of the British and the nation's ingenuity, and that's why it has passed into the modern folklore of the land. The bravery of the bombing raiders was due to the fact that the dams were heavily protected by anti-aircraft emplacements. The ingenuity was due to the fact that in order to breach the dams a whole new type of bomb had to be developed. A bouncing bomb. A bomb that would skip across the surface of the dam-created lake like a

stone skimming across a millpond. (Incidentally, whatever happened to millponds?).

Luckily for us we had just the man for the job. Step
forward the scientist Dr Barnes Wallace.

So heroic a story undoubtedly demanded an equally
heroic tune to get the patriotic blood coursing through
the veins. And that's exactly what the composer Eric
Coates produced when he gave the nation 'The Dam
Busters March'.

The tune went like this:

'Derrr, der, der, derr, de-de, der, der
Derr, der, der, derr, de-de, der, der
Der, d'der, der, der, d'der
Der, d'der, der, der...'

(NB: Obviously this representation of the tune would be
greatly enhanced by knowing the actual music. But if you
don't know the music just ask someone in the street and
they'll be able to point you in the right direction.)

When the movie first hit the cinemas in the 1950s the
patriotically stirred audience would stride purposefully
out into the highways and byways of this still-free
Sceptered Isle with a spring in their step, quietly
humming the tune to themselves in an-ever-so British
state of reticent pride.

Come the 1970s, when the film seemed to be shown
every other bank holiday weekend, the audience became

heavily weighted towards small boys for whom the Second World War was nothing more than an endless succession of adventures in which the plucky British defeated Hitler single-handedly (or with only a bit of help from Clint Eastwood in *Where Eagles Dare*), and Nazis were cruel but smartly dressed, and everyone eventually escaped from Colditz.

And it was in the 1970s that 'The Dam Busters March' acquired actions.

The actions are these:

1   Raise your two hands to your face.
2   Pinch the thumb and first finger of each hand together to form circles.
3   Rest the circles over your eyes while pointing your elbows away from your body.

Now comes the tricky bit.

4   Flip the thumb and finger circles up and over so that the inside of the circles rest over your eyes and your elbows get lifted higher.

(NB: If you're having difficulty mastering this manoeuvre go out into the street again and track down that bloke who helped you with the tune. Incidentally, do make sure it is a bloke that you ask, women are absolutely rubbish when it comes to war movies.)

Once your hands and elbows are in the right position start to defiantly hum 'The Dam Busters March' while slowly twisting from side to side.

Why, exactly, 'The Dam Busters March' acquired actions need not detain us here. Nor should we ponder unduly on the identity of the genius who first matched hand and arm positions to the tune.

All that matters is that the music and movement go hand in hand. (As it were.) Attempt to deconstruct the genesis and meaning of this exclusively British cultural phenomenon and some decidedly revealing revelations are revealed.

Britain likes war nostalgia. Especially if the war being nostalged is the Second World War. Mainly this is because it was the last war of any importance that the country actually won. Admittedly, we did win the Falklands War. But a very wise man said at the time of that particular conflict that it was like two bald men fighting over a comb. No, if Britain wants to feel good about a war, then World War Two is the only can in the cupboard.

Next we hit the second layer of nostalgia. For people too young to have actually been involved in WWII, what 1950s and 1960s films about the conflict conjure up is an era in which Britain still had a reasonably successful and independent film industry and, hence, still had some control over the narrative of the nation's finest hours. Try and remake *The Dam Busters* today, and in order to ensure success in the United States Barnes Wallace would probably have to be portrayed as an introverted geek scientist played by a credibility seeking Owen Wilson.

The third layer of nostalgia is generated by the now middle-aged men who watched it on the telly thirty years ago, and then ran down the park to engage in musically accompanied dogfights with their mates until it got dark and their mums called them in for their teas. (Hoops, usually.)

Then throw in a soupçon of, by now, totally undeserved anti-German sentiment. And finally add in a dash of self-deprecation that tacitly acknowledges it is patently absurd to still be going on about this stuff sixty years after the end of the war, and you begin to get to grips with the Britishness of it all.

But even as you do, the chances are that it will squirm out of your grasp. That's because in any culture that is alive and kicking the meaning of stuff is constantly changing.

All of which brings us to Highbury Football ground one cold, damp winter's evening in 2003. Highbury was the home of Arsenal, a team at the time that played some of the most beautiful football ever seen in this country. A key architect of the wonders was the Dutchman Dennis Bergkamp. The visitors on this occasion were a Chelsea football club as yet not bloated on the cash mountain of an unimaginably wealthy Russian oligarch. As such, if Chelsea were to succeed they would have to rely on the skill of what players they could afford. And the wit of their supporters.

While the players may have regularly underperformed, the supporters didn't. And the man that they had singled out for their attentions this night was Mr D. Bergkamp. A Mr D. Bergkamp who, as well being the scorer of blissfully sublime goals, was also famed for refusing to step foot on an aeroplane ever since a terrifying incident while travelling abroad with the Dutch national youth team.

Seven minutes into the game Bergkamp hares towards the Clock End and the visitor's goal, to the right of which are the massed ranks of Chelsea's supporters. To a man, the blue bedecked fans rise to their feet, lift their hands to their eyes, stick their elbows out, gently sway from side to side and launch into:

'Derr, der, der, derr, de-de, der, der
Derr, der, der, derr, de-de, der, der
Der, d'der, der, der, d'der
Der, d'der, der, der…'

One–nil to Chelsea.

Now, if you're beginning to get an inkling of all the many paths that came together in that particular, glorious crossroads of a moment, then you're beginning to understand what a wonderfully complex thing it is to be British.

~ 23 ~

*Having driven for many hours,
probably on a bank holiday,
to enjoy the delights of a famous
beauty spot, where is the most
British place to eat your sandwiches?*

In the car park.

~ 24 ~

What is the correct British demeanour to effect when commuting to work?

The correct demeanour to effect when commuting to work is resigned sullenness.

On no account should any visible sign of happiness, levity or even contentment ever sully your brow. Indeed smile at anyone and you might as well don an oversized, Katharine Hamnett-style T-shirt, emblazoned with the legend 'I AM A FOREIGNER. I DON'T BELONG HERE'.

If all this sounds a little unfriendly then you are completely misunderstanding a key part of the British psyche. That's because, for the typical Briton, commuting to work is only partly about the physical journey. The far more important journey being undertaken is the psychological transition from being 'at home' to being 'at work'. So the commute to work is an opportunity for the commuter to get themselves into the right frame of mind to 'work'.

To fully understand how intense an experience this can be we need to step out of the Arena Of Commuting and draw a parallel with a scene played out at the Barcelona Olympic Games in 1992.

The occasion is, arguably, the premier event of any Olympiad – the final of the men's one hundred metres. The subject we are considering is Linford Christie. Observe him closely and even before he steps up to the blocks he has shut himself in a world of his own. His eyes stare straight ahead of him, focused with an intensity that is awesome to contemplate. There is only one thing in his mind. To get to the end of the hundred-metre track before anyone else. Indeed, so intense is his focus, that it's easy to believe he may not even be aware there is anyone else on the track with him.

It's just him and his destiny.

Given this state of affairs, it's very unlikely he would have welcomed anyone nearby smiling amicably at him and trying to engage him in cheery banter about the latest goings-on down at the Queen Vic.

The average Briton on their way to work is likewise in a similar zone of focus. It's just that they haven't quite mastered the external display of intensity that Linford went in for. Which is just as well as whole train carriages full of people who looked as fearsome as Linford did on the hundred-metre track at Barcelona would truly be a terrifying prospect for anyone trying to board the train at the next station.

Instead, British commuters have learned to mask their intensity with an outward display of resigned sullenness. It is a facade of indifference that clearly signals to those in the know (i.e., fellow commuters) that, involved as they are in their own psychological transition from the state of being 'at home' to the state of being 'at work', they really do not want to engage in any form of social interaction whatsoever.

Should you want to blend into British society you should learn to do the same. And whatever you do don't smile. Ever.

~ 25 ~

The Krays were notorious gangsters and murderers. What, in the popular British imagination, excused their crimes?

Yes, the Krays were involved in theft, extortion, violence and killing, but they weren't that bad because 'they only hurt their own kind'.

On the face of it, there may appear to be some kind of merit in such thinking. Even if it is wishful thinking. The

A right pair

implication of the logic being that if you as an individual did not get involved in criminality, then the Krays and their gang would not get involved in your life. Sadly, this betrays a somewhat naïve view of how criminals actually work. And what is really at play here is a peculiarly British form of nostalgia. It is a nostalgia that paints the reassuring picture that even crime was better in the old days.

The other flaw in this thinking can be seen if one extends the principle a tad further. If it's acceptable for gangsters to kill other gangsters, then is it acceptable for accountants to kill other accountants, chiropodists to kill other chiropodists, and – if the provocation has been severe enough – lollipop ladies to kill other lollipop ladies?

~ 26 ~

What is 'binge thinking'?

Binge thinking is when groups of politicians, usually lads, get together and keep on thinking late into the night, having one idea after another, ending up in a right mess. They then stagger onto the streets mouthing off to all and sundry that they know how to do things. Often they're spoiling for a fight. But they're so inebriated with all the thinks that they've thunk they invariably come a cropper.

One recent example of binge thinking is when Mr Cameron, leader of the Conservative Party, got together with his mates and decided that his party would not advocate the building of any more grammar schools. Unfortunately, in the cold light of day, this policy began to look a touch bleary-eyed and decidedly wobbly-legged. Little wonder then that Mr Cameron soon found himself having to change direction and totter back in the direction he had just came from.

Unfortunately, this bout of binge thinking also led to an equally unedifying spectacle on the Labour Party benches in Parliament where many, who should know better, indulged in a long bout of passive smirking.

~ 27 ~

How has the way that Britain sees itself changed from Shakespeare's time to our own?

This is how William Shakespeare saw our nation in Act II, Scene I of his play *Richard II*:

> This royal throne of kings, this scepter'd isle,
> This earth of majesty, this seat of Mars,
> This other Eden, demi-paradise,
> This fortress built by nature for herself,
> Against infection and the hand of war,
> This happy breed of men, this little world,
> This precious stone set in the silver sea,
> Which serves it in the office of a wall,
> Or as a moat defensive to a house,
> Against the envy of less happier lands,
> This blessed plot, this earth, this realm, this
> England...

Obviously since those embarrassingly naïve days our understanding of our own nationhood has moved on quite a bit and is far more sophisticated!

The following is taken from the start of *Life in the United Kingdom: A Journey to Citizenship*. It is 'The Official Publication. Published on behalf of the Life in the United Kingdom Advisory Group'. And is produced by the Home Office which is, reassuringly, 'Building A Safe, Just And Tolerant Society'.

'The name of our country on British passports is "The United Kingdom of Great Britain and Northern Ireland". This refers to the union of what were once four separate countries: England, Scotland, Wales, and Ireland (though most of Ireland is now independent). Most people, however, say, "Britain" or "Great Britain". Usually "Britain" refers to the mainland and "Great Britain" includes Northern Ireland, and also the Channel Islands and the Isle Of Man who have different institutions of government. But even the British can get confused with these different names and usages. Scots and Welsh, if asked, "What is your citizenship?" will correctly say "British", and if asked, "What is your nationality?" they will almost always reply "Scottish" or "Welsh". But the native-born English, outnumbering the others by nine to one, will often give the same answer to both questions, as if his or her nationality as well as citizenship was British. So in the United Kingdom national identity and a strong and proud sense of citizenship are not always the same thing.'

Stirring stuff indeed!

~ 28 ~

*You go out for a meal with friends
or colleagues. When the bill comes
how much should you pay?*

In Britain the conventional approach is to split the bill evenly between all the people in the party. So if the total bill is £100 and there are 10 of you in the group just divide 100 by 10 and the result would be that every person pays £10. Obviously in reality the mathematics is rarely this simple. (Or the restaurants this reasonable.)

What may not be apparent until you actually find yourself involved in such a scenario is that this method of resolving the situation is inevitably unfair. After all, how likely is it that every person in the group ate food and drank drinks that cost the same amount as every other person? So in any group restaurant visit some people will be getting a far better deal than others and, more significantly, some will be getting a far worse deal.

The obvious solution would be for everybody to pay for what they ate and drank. The downside of this is that it requires each individual to request a separate bill before the food and drink is ordered. Or it needs a complex napkin arithmetic session once the composite bill has arrived at the end of the meal. Neither approach can be said to be conducive to the general bonhomie of the occasion.

Despite this, you may often find in any one party that there is one individual who will insist on only paying for what they ate, and far more irritatingly, knowing and itemising what everyone else ate and hence how much more than themselves they should pay. Strangely these people are often the ones who earn far more than anyone else. And they are frequently called Bruce.

The real crux of the financial dilemma is most commonly about drink. This is because while it is relatively rare for individuals in a group to eat vastly different amounts of food, it is quite common for individuals to drink vastly different amounts of alcohol. And it is the cost of the alcohol before, during and after a meal that can turn what seemed to be a reasonably-priced restaurant when you examined the menu in the window, into a pocket-emptying exercise by the time you make it back on to the street.

If you are a non-drinker your best hope is that someone else in the group will speak up on your behalf and suggest that maybe you shouldn't pay as much as everyone else as you 'didn't drink anything'. Alternatively, you could point out this fact. This, however, takes a certain degree of social courage and is best only attempted if you are sure of your standing and acceptance within the group. Otherwise you run the risk of being thought of as a bit of a 'Bruce'. The other solution would be to compensate for the impending bill discrepancy by either ordering for yourself the most expensive dishes on the menu or a lot more food than anyone else. However this may well result in you being thought of as a greedy pig by the drunkards you've gone out with.

All of which leads us to the quite surprising, but undoubtedly British, after-effect of having gone out for a meal with colleagues or friends. The problem is, that no matter how poorly or, indeed, how well the whole bill issue is resolved, you will often be left with the lingering doubt that you have ended up paying more than you should have. Inevitably, this means you will find yourself resenting the people you've just been out with. Your colleagues. Your friends. Or, in extreme cases, your partner. (Admittedly if you do find yourself feeling this it may well be symptomatic of far more fundamental problems in your relationship.)

However, the true test of Britishness is how you handle this petty resentment. The preferred British option is not to say anything. Because you 'don't want to make a fuss'.

Now, is anyone going to have a pudding?

*In Britain, how soon after a
contestant has won a TV reality
show is it permissible to lose
all interest in them?*

One week. Or, if the show has been a 'singing' contest, by the time their second single is released. Extend your interest beyond this time and you run the risk of being branded, to a greater or lesser degree, as somewhat sad.

The one-week rule applies because no matter how riveting you found the individual concerned while they were involved in the contest, by one week after they have won you will come to realise it was the unreal setting of the 'contest' that generated much of the interest.

Also, a week into the post-contest period and one of the key anomalies of the whole reality genre kicks in. The people who win these shows – invariably decided by viewers votes – aren't necessarily the best, or the most talented, but tend to be the most likeable. Coupled with this is the fact that the people watching also want somebody with whom they can identify. They want the winners to be, to a certain extent, 'just like them'. (And, obviously, some kind of childhood hardship or family tragedy doesn't go amiss either.)

But the anomaly is that after the show is over, like-ability and being 'just like' the viewer, the very things that won them the show in the first place, become the things that cause the viewer to lose interest. After all, do we really want our pop stars to be 'likeable' and 'just like us'? Even worse, before long their very ordinariness, coupled with the fact that whoever is 'managing' the winner will want them to cash in on their success, often leads to an unpleasant undercurrent of resentment.

So, whereas large parts of the British public started off thinking the winners should have success because they're 'just like me', they end up thinking why should they have so much 'success' if they're 'just like me'. That's why, when the one-time winners crash and burn, their demise can be greeted with a degree of satisfaction.

Given all this, a post-contest shelf life of only one week is totally understandable. Also, it's in the week after the win that the tabloid newspapers who haven't snapped up the winner's 'EXCLUSIVE STORY!' unleash the dirt they've dug up about the winner, their family or how badly they treated their ex-lover's pet gerbil that time they were supposed to be looking after it.

~ 30 ~

What is the significance of Sollershott Circus?

Sollershott Circus in Letchworth, Hertfordshire was, in 1910, the first traffic roundabout to be opened in Britain. However it wasn't until 1929 and the Ministry of Transport circular no 302 that the word 'roundabout' appeared for the first time, when it was recommended that 'spaces should be provided for traffic to circulate on the "roundabout" system'. The next quantum leap in round-about design had to wait almost fifty years, for the 1970s. That's when the mini-roundabout started to appear.

Currently there are around about three-and-a-half thousand roundabouts in England alone.

Perhaps the most sought-after of roundabout memo-rabilia is the 2002 calendar *Roundabouts of Redditch* produced by BB Print Digital in Worcestershire.

~ 31 ~

What is the difference between a 'dog's dinner' and 'the dog's bollocks'?

Obviously, to a dog, there is a big difference.

Less obviously, however, to your average British citizen there is quite a lot of difference too.

The expression a 'dog's dinner' or even a 'complete dog's dinner' is used to indicate something that has been made into an extremely unappealing mess. For example, it could be said that the Millenium Dome project in Greenwich was a 'complete dog's dinner'. In contrast to describe something as 'the dog's bollocks' is to accord it a very high accolade indeed. For example, when the Millenium Dome project was championed in Parliament by Mr Tony Blair, while he didn't actually say that it was going to be 'the dog's bollocks' this was, clearly, the picture he was painting as to the intended nature of the folly.

Interestingly, when the whole thing went decidedly pear-shaped four other canine based words or phrases could be used to describe what went on. First the press wouldn't stop hounding the scheme. Then Mr Blair defended the project doggedly. And finally, realising he was on a hiding to nothing, he sloped off from the scene, with his tail between his legs, while muttering the political equivalent of having 'to see a man about a dog'.

Newcomers to Britain should note, however, that while 'the dog's bollocks' is high praise indeed, it is not a phrase used in polite society. Should you ever find yourself in such circumstances and encounter difficulties in coming up with a suitable simile, you could do a lot worse than describing the thing in question as being 'pure pedigree'. However if you were to add the seemingly friendly familiarity of the word 'chum' to the end of your compliment, you will have made a 'complete dog's dinner' of it.

~ 32 ~

*In Britain is it permissible for
small, unsupervised, children to ask
strangers on the street for money
with which to buy explosives?*

Unfortunately it is getting less and less permissible. Which is a shame. It used to happen in the autumn in the weeks leading up to November the fifth. The explosives in question are fireworks and they would be bought to be set off as part of Guy Fawkes/Bonfire Night celebrations.

Traditionally the money for the fireworks would be raised by the making, from old clothes stuffed with newspapers, of a 'guy' – an effigy of Mr Fawkes – that would be propped against a wall on a street. The small child who had made the guy would then accost adult passers-by with the plaintive demand of:

'Penny for the guy, mister.'

The passing adult would then look down at the guy, secretly think to himself that he used to make a much better one than that when he was a kid, but then plunge his hand into his pocket and deposit the loose change he found there into the proffered hat. At the end of the day the small child would count up his takings and, with Fagin-like glee, work out in his head just how many explosives he could buy.

The whole performance would be repeated several times in the days leading up to the big night. The actual buying of the fireworks would be an occasion of great excitement. Old biscuit tins full of accumulated change would be tipped across the counter of the newspaper shop that sold the fireworks and carefully counted out with all the concentration and diligence of a new Chancellor of the Exchequer allocating funds to the various government departments before his first Budget speech to the House of Commons. So much would go towards rockets, so much towards Roman candles, so much towards Catherine wheels, and of course there'd also have to be a packet or two of sparklers. And, somehow, there'd always be enough money left over to buy the undoubted ASBO family of the firework community, a box of bangers.

Once purchased, the fireworks would be taken home to be stored in a safe box, in a safe place, not to be touched until the big night. Obviously the 'not to be touched' bit was a case of wishful thinking. Because what small child could resist the temptation to sneakily, when their parents were watching telly, make their way to the 'safe place' and get down and open the 'safe box' and, like an awestruck believer cautiously handling a revered relic of a medieval saint, contemplate the wonder and joy and glorification of the heavens that these simple objects would soon provide?

Being shouted at by your parents to 'leave the fireworks alone!' was also an essential part of the annual ritual. But there were other elements too, without which the whole experience would not be the same. For a start there was the expression on the faces of the *Blue Peter* presenters as they told you that while Guy Fawkes night was great fun, fireworks could be dangerous and so they should be handled properly. The expression was a serious, I-know-you-can-be-responsible one, that subliminally delivered into a million child-filled living rooms the message that, sadly, there's more to life than sticky-backed plastic. There was the exciting, but slightly perturbing, instruction 'Light the blue touchpaper, then retire'. (Retire? You hadn't even got a job. You were only nine.) There was the half-remembered rhyme 'Remember, remember, the fifth of November, gunpowder treason and plot'. There was the debate about whether to have the firework party on the night of the fifth itself, or at the weekend, or would that clash with the council/boy scout/church display so no one would come? And there was the annual discussion about what food to have, which always ended up with the annual answer of baked potatoes, soup and sausages.

And, of course, there was the Firework Safety Code with its command of commands 'Never Throw Fireworks'. Accompanying this, in every playground in the land, would be small huddles of small children gathered together to listen in wide-eyed fascination to the story of so-and-so's cousin who was playing outside when some big boys came and joined in and started throwing bangers at each other and one went off right in so-and-so's cousin's face and HE LOST AN EYE!

The morning after the night itself the walk to school would be enlivened by the collection of the fallen wooden sticks that such a short time before had whizzed heavenwards from a million back-garden milk-bottle Cape Canaverals. And after school you'd always have to examine the still fence-post pinned remnants of a now rain-soaked Catherine wheel that briefly spun around showering the world in glowing golden embers before getting stuck and burning itself out.

But these days all this has become very much a thing of the past.

Small children begging strangers on the street for money to buy explosives are no longer the winter equivalent of the first swallow of summer. And fewer and fewer people have a firework party in their back gardens any more. Consequently a whole new generation of so-and-so's cousins can face the future with a full complement of eyes. Which can't be a bad thing.

Except, maybe, that by making Britain's children safer we have robbed them of an opportunity of intangible worth. After all, back in the day while so-and-so's cousin may well have lost an eye, the vast majority of cousins didn't. And that's because the even vaster majority of children did not throw fireworks. And maybe that's because handling something so obviously dangerous as fireworks taught the children of Britain valuable lessons in how to be responsible.

But maybe the current thinking is that it would be irresponsible for us to give our children this chance to be responsible. Better we keep them in a 'safe box' and keep that in a 'safe place' and only get them out when there's an adult around to make sure no one gets hurt. Ever. The only problem is that this could leave us with a generation of molly-coddled damp squibs. And then what should we do when we eventually light the blue touchpaper and retire and nothing happens?

After all, as everyone knows, you should never return to a firework once it's lit. Even if it doesn't go off.

Whilst the decline in Street Corner Small Child–Adult Stranger Begging For Money For Explosives interfaces in contemporary Britain is one that any sensible Briton must surely lament, the whole scenario does highlight another aspect of our lives that has clearly changed for the better. Very few of our younger generations know much about Guy Fawkes. This is because there has been a far-sighted decision taken to downplay the importance of teaching history to our youngsters. As is patently clear to anyone with a brain, teaching history is fundamentally rooted in the past and backward looking. Clearly what we in general, and our youth in particular, need to do is to look ahead. To the future.

Just by coincidence there can be no better way to illustrate this point than to consider the story of Guy Fawkes and to see how it is of absolutely no relevance to anything that is going on in our great nation today.

Fawkes was born at Stonegate in Yorkshire in 1570. Raised as a Protestant, his father died when he was young. His mother remarried into the Bainbridge family, who were Catholic. When he was sixteen Guy converted to Catholicism. This was a decision not without serious consequences at the time as Catholics were subject to disapproval, discrimination and legal sanctions. The situation worsened when James I succeeded to the throne of England.

As a young man Guy travelled to the Netherlands to join the army of Archduke Albert of Austria that was fighting with the armies of Catholic Spain against the Protestant United Provinces. This was fundamentally a religious war, with the Dutch trying to resist the imposition of Spain's ruling Catholic Inquisition on the Low Countries. In the years of conflict Guy, who had changed his name to Guido, learned military discipline and how to handle explosives.

On his return to England his knowledge of military matters and explosives led to him being co-opted into the conspiracy that would eventually be known as the Gunpowder Plot. While he might have been, in many ways, the leader of the plot, he wasn't the mastermind behind it. That accolade fell to Robert Catesby, who conceived the idea of killing King James the First, along with members of his family, and his ministers of state, who had gathered to witness the official opening of Parliament.

The plot was prompted by the realisation that Spain was too militarily stretched, and in too much debt, to come to the aid of the persecuted English Catholics. It was a situation exacerbated by a conference in 1604 where the king further attacked the Catholics.

To execute their plans the plotters rented out a cellar under the House of Lords. Over the course of many weeks they smuggled in thirty-six barrels of gunpowder. To disguise the barrels they were covered over with stacked wood. The scheme only failed because some of the conspirators had an attack of conscience. Kind of. They realised that amongst those who would be killed in the explosion would be fellow Catholics who were trying to fight their cause through Parliament. A letter of warning was sent to Lord Monteagle, one of the Catholics at risk. He passed it on to the authorities.

On November the Fifth, the cellars of the House of Lords were searched and Guy Fawkes was discovered nearby with all that he needed to light the fuse for the explosion. Fawkes later declared that had he been in the cellar at the time it was searched by Sir Thomas Knyvett he would have 'blown him up, house, himself and all'.

Guy Fawkes, who first gave his name as John Johnson, was tortured for four days without giving much away. Eventually he revealed only the names of those

A terrorist

already dead or already known to the authorities. On the 31st of January he was tried, hung, drawn and quartered.

A witness to the events wrote the following:

'Last of all came the great devil of all, Guy Fawkes, alias Johnson, who should have put fire to the powder. His body being weak with torture and sickness he was scarce able to go up the ladder, yet with much ade, by the help of the hangman, went high enough to break his neck by the fall. He made no speech, but with his crosses and idle ceremonies made his end upon the gallows and the block, to the great joy of all the beholders that the land was ended so wicked a villainy.'

In the years that followed the tradition was established of the parading of an effigy around the town on the anniversary of the plot. An effigy that would be subsequently burnt on a bonfire. And children would chant rhymes to celebrate the foiling of so murderous an attack.

> *'Remember, remember the Fifth of November,*
> *Gunpowder, treason and plot,*
> *I know of no reason why the Gunpowder Treason*
> *Should ever be forgot.'*

The rhyme subsequently goes on to explain the plot. But it ends by attacking the force that was seen as the real enemy.

> *'A penny loaf to feed the Pope.*
> *A farthing o'cheese to choke him.*
> *A pint of beer to rinse it down.*
> *A faggot of sticks to burn him.*
> *Burn him in a tub of tar.*
> *Burn him like a blazing star.*
> *Burn his body from his head.*
> *Then we'll say ol' Pope is dead*
> *Hip hip hoorah*
> *Hip hip hoorah hoorah!'*

What's more, there is evidence to suggest that the effigy that was originally paraded and burnt was not Guy Fawkes, but the Pope. And some argue that it wasn't until as late as 1806 that the leader of the Catholic Church in Rome was replaced by Guy Fawkes atop the nation's bonfires.

Obviously none of this has any relevance to, nor can shed any light upon, anything that's happening in Britain today.

So clearly the demise of history in the nation's national curriculum can only be a good thing as it frees up more time for Media Studies. Or, as Gerald Ford so succinctly put it:

'History is bunk.'

~ 33 ~

Can you arrange the following British curries in order of hotness?

A. Madras
B. Vindaloo
C. Korma
D. Tikka Masala
E. Edwina

The correct order in ascending degree of heat is:

1. Korma
2. Tikka Masala
3. Madras
4. Vindaloo

NB: the last 'curry' on the list is a trick. Edwina Currie is not an actual dish but a person. Well, she is a person now, but she used to be a politician. She was a Conservative government minister who's claim to fame rested on questioning the safety of British eggs during one of the country's periodic food crises.

Subsequent claims by Mrs Currie revealed that her somewhat scrambled thinking may, in part, have been due to the confusion caused by serving as agriculture minister 'under' a Prime Minister who proclaimed the importance of 'family values' whilst simultaneously making sure that his interest in her briefs wasn't solely confined to how eggs were being laid.

~ 34 ~

What is the point of the Boat Race?

The point of the Boat Race is to see whether Oxford University or Cambridge University is better at rowing. The real question, however, is why this should be of any interest to anyone outside the universities themselves?

After all, rowing is a minority sport. And going to Oxford or Cambridge is a minority, albeit a highly influential minority, way of pissing away the years between school and work. And it's not even as if the way the Boat Race plays out is a particularly riveting sporting contest. Essentially one boat gets ahead of the other fairly early on and stays there until the end of the race. And the race takes around twenty minutes. So for a good eighteen of those twenty minutes very little happens. Consequently, there's very little to watch. Occasional 'drama' occurs should, in the early stages, the boats get too close to each other. Then there's the risk of oars clashing. Briefly. Should the conditions on the river be a bit rough, there's also the slim possibility that one of the boats might sink.

Unfortunately this has happened only once in living memory when Leonardo DiCaprio, who was rowing in a boat that Kate Winslett was coxing in, ended up drowning. (In retrospect this sounds quite unlikely, and it could well be that the entire nation had nodded off in front of the TV coverage of the race and only woken up to catch the end of the movie *Titanic*.)

All of which will lead yourself, as an inquisitive newcomer to this country, to ask that if the Boat Race is a decidedly dire spectacle as a sporting contest, and that most of the country couldn't give a toss about the rivalry between Oxford University and Cambridge University, then why is the thing a permanent fixture on the sports broadcasting calendar and one accorded such a high degree of reverence?

To understand the answer to this question one must contemplate the fundamental nature of the contest. And of the coverage of it.

The Boat Race is a sporting contest in which very little happens. And yet the commentators must find things to say to keep the viewer engaged. So they talk about the weather. The conditions 'on the water'. The make-up of the crews. The weights of the coxes. The parents of the coxes. The weights of the parents of the coxes. The history of the Race. The traditions. The superstitions. The people who crowd the embankments to watch. The bridges the boats go under. The pubs that line the course. Indeed anything at all they can conjure up to disguise the fact that for the vast majority of the 'race' bugger all of any interest is going on.

Now why this should be of vital importance to the nation is this. The Boat Race, in which very little of interest happens, lasts twenty minutes. A cricket Test match, on the other hand, can last five days. And after that it often ends in a draw. So the Boat Race, and the coverage of it, has long been a way of acclimatising viewers to sporting events in which nothing happens. And it is a way of subliminally establishing within the broadcasting community the skills and aptitudes needed to commentate on supposedly riveting contests when very little is going on.

The veracity of this analysis is confirmed by the fact that, until very recently, both the coverage of The Boat Race and Test match cricket were in the hands of the BBC. In the past few years, however, the rights to cover Test match cricket has been bought by Sky Sports, while The Boat Race has been nabbed by ITV. All of which might lead the newcomer to this country to worry that the BBC's great tradition of providing commentaries for contests where nothing much is going on might soon be restricted to the rain breaks at Wimbledon. But luckily for all us, and especially for the BBC, that vast repository of skills developed over years of Boat Race coverage on knowing what to say about an elitist contest when there's very little actual conflict going on, and both sides look pretty much the same anyway, can easily be transferred to the coverage of politics in Britain.

~ 35 ~

What relationship should Bob be to you to have things, all of a sudden and for no apparent reason, work out for the best?

Bob should be your uncle.

That's because 'Bob's your uncle' is a phrase commonly employed by the people of Britain when things, all of a sudden, work out for the best.

For example, a humble titan of industry might say 'I just happened to have donated a million pounds to the Labour Party before the last election when, Bob's your uncle, I found myself with a seat in the House Of Lords!'

The origin of the phrase dates back to the 1886 promotion of Arthur Balfour to the position of Secretary of State for Ireland. It was an appointment that came as a considerable surprise. Then people picked up on the fact that Balfour's uncle was Robert Gascoyne-Cecil, a man who, at the time, just happened to be Prime Minister.

~ 36 ~

Who ate all the pies?

The question is a rhetorical one. It is also a sung one. That is because what we are dealing with here is a football chant. A football chant is a chant chanted at a football match by the supporters of a particular team. The lyrical gist of a chant may exhort the skills of their team, the hardness of their fans, or the magical qualities of their team's manager. The chants can also pour scorn and derision on their opponents. Their opponents' fans. Their opponents' ground. Or even on their opponents' manager's mother's marital fidelity.

Given all this, the chant 'Who ate all the pies?' is a relatively innocent form of melodic abuse. The melody that the query is sung to being the tune of 'Knees-Up Mother Brown'. 'Who ate all the pies?' is usually directed at any player of the opposing team who appears to be even slightly overweight. In its commonest form the question is sung twice before the denouement of the song is delivered with relish. The denouement being

> *You fat bastard!*
> *You fat bastard!*

You ate all the pies!'

Obviously this is not exactly an example of Wildean wit, but it does make its point both effectively and with admirable brevity.

For any aspirant Briton a knowledge of the basics of football chantery is both useful and informative. If nothing else, it gives an insight into the functioning of a particularly British, self-defining, and self-contained society. Beyond that there is the added bonus that if one attends a football match, and joins in with the chants, for however long that chant lasts you are part of, and will be accepted as part of, that society.

Other key football chants that you should really be au fait with include:

> *'Sing when you're winning!*
> *You only sing when you're winning!*
> *Sing when you're winning!*
> *You only sing when you're winning!'*

Which is sung to the tune of 'Guantanamera' and used when the opposition fans, who had been in full song when their team were ahead, fall into silence when the other side equalises or goes into the lead.

In a similar vein, and similar circumstances, an equalising goal may well prompt celebrating fans to taunt their rivals with the words:

'You're not singing,
You're not singing,
You're not singing any more
You're not singing any more'

Which is belted out to the tune of the hymn 'Guide Me Oh Thy Great Redeemer'.

General derision of an opposing team's performance is often signalled by the use of the Village People tune 'Go West' with the lyrics amended to read:

'You're shit and you know you are...'

Chants can also be specific to specific teams. Perhaps the most famous being 'You'll Never Walk Alone' which is the unofficial anthem of Liverpool football team, and more specifically the Kop End of Anfield. The song is taken from Rodgers & Hammerstein's 1945 musical *Carousel*. It was adopted by The Kop in the early 1960s after the Merseybeat group Gerry and The Pacemakers had a hit with it in 1963. The refrain, as sung by The Kop, can also be found on the atmospheric fade-out of what is, arguably, Pink Floyd's most beautiful song, 'Fearless', on their 1971 album *Meddle*.

The most lyrical and philosophical football chant, however, undoubtedly belongs to West Ham. Their song 'I'm Forever Blowing Bubbles' is not a hymn to their club's skills or glory, instead it is a contemplation on the fleeting nature of dreams. Thirty thousand voices raised in unison singing:

> *'I'm forever blowing bubbles*
> *Pretty bubbles in the air*
> *They float so high*
> *They reach the sky*
> *Then like my dreams they fade and die...'*

as the team in claret and blue underperform yet again, is a thing of wonder.

As for the wit of the football chant, that's to be found at almost every ground. For example back in the 1979–1980 season Liverpool came up against lowly Grimsby in the third round of the FA Cup. The match, as a contest, was over by half-time with Liverpool eventually winning 5–0. As the Grimsby fans lapsed into silence the Liverpool faithful laid into them with the now legendary jibe:

> *'Sing when you're fishing,*
> *You only sing when you're fishing...'*

A cod

Self-deprecation can also be found in the most unlikely of places. The much-disliked Millwall accepted the animosity with which they are often viewed and channelled it into a version of Rod Stewart's 'Sailing' that proudly proclaimed:

'No one likes us,
No one likes us,
No one likes us,
We don't care...'

While Barnsley FC managed to pull off the seemingly impossible feat of combining self-deprecation with hyperbole when they started to proclaim to the tune of 'Blue Moon':

'Brazil,
It's just like watching Brazil...'

But perhaps the real genius of the football chant lies in its ability to topically respond to a specific set of circumstances. Once the circumstances change, the chant is in reality no longer relevant, but its power is such that it can live on in the collective subconscious of a disparate group of individuals who periodically come together to worship at one of the shrines of the national game.

Back in the early days of Arsene Wenger's reign at Arsenal one of his biggest successes was the teenager

Nicolas Anelka. Anelka had talent to burn but an attitude that soon had him sulking off towards the supposed glamour of Real Madrid. One of the players Wenger bought to replace him was the Nigerian striker Nwankwo Kanu.

A few weeks into the Nigerian's time at Highbury the terraces reverberated with a brand-new anthem:

> *'Chim-chimeree,*
> *Chim-chimeree,*
> *Chim-chim cheroo!*
> *Who needs Anelka,*
> *When we've got Kanu!'*

How can Britain not be a great country when our citizens can come up with stuff like that?

~ 37 ~

*Where do the gannet and the kingfisher
join forces to protect the British Isles?*

Within the pages of the new, biometric British passports.
They are the watermarks of the paper used in the passports to help prevent forgery.

Other birds featured in the passport include the
curlew, the red kite, the merlin and the avocet.

And the electronic chip that contains the biometric
data on the person whose passport it is can be found on
a page featuring an illustration of a stool pigeon.

~ 38 ~

How much of the Concorde did the French actually design?

Very little.

~ 39 ~

What is a 'Chinese burn'? And how, if at all, does it differ from a 'Rabbie Burns'?

A 'Chinese burn' is a common childhood torture inflicted by one urchin on another in British playgrounds, well out of the sight of whichever member of staff is on playground duty. To inflict a 'Chinese burn' on an enemy the perpetrator first must grab his victim's forearm with both his hands. He then tightens his grip on the bare skin whilst simultaneously twisting his hands in opposing directions. The tighter the grip, the higher the level of pain inflicted.

By tradition 'Chinese burns' tend to be employed in the latter years of primary school, and perhaps in the first year of secondary school. To still be using 'Chinese burns' beyond that age is generally frowned upon and thought to indicate a severe lack of bullying imagination. Thankfully, in these modern times, technology has loaned a helping hand to the older bully by inventing what some cognescenti describe as the 'iPod of abuse': Happy Slapping.

What is interesting to note is that the 'Chinese burn' is, by and large, a male form of bullying. Boys give

'Chinese burns' to other boys. As such it is always a 'one-on-one' affair. Girls on the other hand tend to eschew the, frankly, childish physical simplicity of the 'Chinese burn' when they round on a victim, and instead favour the sophisticated complexity of group politics and social ostracism. Once again technology has enabled the young British female bully to move with the times thanks to the advent of anonymous text messaging and computer-based cyber-bullying.

Why the 'Chinese burn' should be Chinese has never been adequately explained.

A 'Rabbie Burns' is not a form of childhood torture at all. He is, in fact, Scotland's national poet. He wrote his poems in Scottish dialect. Amongst his most famous is 'Address To A Haggis' which, by tradition, is recited on Burns Night each year as a haggis, held high on a plate, is led to a table of seated, and often kilted, diners. The 'great chieftain o' the puddin-race' is serenaded to its place by the bagpipes. A haggis is a traditional delicacy made from the lining of a sheep's stomach stuffed with minced offal mixed with oatmeal. It is an acquired taste. The bagpipes is a wind instrument made from a bag, carried under the arm, out of which pipes extrude that make a distinctive wailing sound. It too is an acquired taste.

Interestingly the 'Chinese burn' is not as common a form of playground torture for boys in Scotland as it is in the rest of Britain. But then again Scottish boys do have the Scottish national football team regularly inflicted upon them, and in many ways that is like a never-ending 'Chinese burn' that gets handed down from one generation to the next.

~ 40 ~

What makes 'Disgusted of Tunbridge Wells' so unhappy?

Almost everything.

That's because almost everything is different to how it used to be. And change is not something that Disgusted enjoys. He would like things to remain as they are. For ever. Or better still, he would like things to change back to the way they were. That's because the way things were, as Barbra Streisand can attest, were infinitely better than the way things are now.

For a more philosophical man, such feelings would manifest themselves as nostalgia. But the man from Tunbridge Wells is not a philosophical man. He is a Man Of Action. Hence the anger.

But, in truth, he isn't really a Man of Action, he only likes to think of himself as such. That's why the only action he ever takes is to lift pen to paper to complain. While this may seem to paint 'Disgusted of Tunbridge Wells' in a somewhat unflattering light, the larger truth is that his persona is, in fact, a part of every Briton's character.

To a great extent this explains why Britain is, historically speaking, a relatively stable society and has never much gone in for revolutions. We are a nation that, in reality, is less likely to man the barricades, than to complain that the barricades aren't built anywhere near as well as the barricades that were built when we were young.

Or look at it from another angle, if things really are so bad in Tunbridge Wells surely 'Disgusted' would move somewhere else.

~ 41 ~

Why did the sun never set on the British Empire?

This was a phrase that gained prominence at the time when Britain's imperial conquests spanned vast parts of the globe. What the phrase described was the fact that the Empire was so extensive that at any time, in any given twenty-four-hour period, somewhere across the globe the sun would be shining on a land governed by the British. Later on the phrase was also taken to indicate the at-the-time self-evident truth that the British Empire would last for ever.

Obviously things have changed quite a bit since then.

Mind you, given recent alterations to retail laws, and the introduction of twenty-four-hour opening, the British nation can still proudly proclaim that 'the sun never sets on the Tesco Empire'.

~ 42 ~

What is the best biscuit to dunk in a cup of tea?

The best biscuit to dunk in a cup of tea is, by near universal consensus, a McVitie's digestive. But in your time in Britain you will often come across people who adamantly protest their allegiance to an alternative. Though their passion is genuine, statistically speaking, they are unrepresentative of the UK dunking fraternity as a whole. You may also encounter individuals (often called Gail) who abhor the whole biscuit-tea-dunk experience. They are clearly misguided. And if they can get so fundamental a matter so horribly wrong, it would only be circumspect to question their judgement on a wide range of other affairs.

The digestive is the dunking biscuit of choice for generation upon generation of tea-imbibing Britons primarily because it has what scientists have quantified as the highest WFI quotient* of all the commonly available British biscuits. This was calibrated in a series of exhaustive tests in which all the biscuits being examined were dunked

---

* Won't Fall In quotient.

in a cup of tea for periods of time that increased in half-second increments. Then the biscuit was removed from the tea. The test was deemed to have been completed when the lifted sodden biscuit, emerging *Mary Rose*-like from the depths, fell apart and sank to the bottom of the mug of tea to sludge about unpleasantly waiting for a soul hardy enough to drain the dregs of the drink.

(Incidentally, this publicly funded investigation shows that not all the research that the government pays for from the collective coffers is bad value for money as it was ingeniously completed by the scientists during tea breaks taken in the course of other projects they were working on. Recent accusations that the research was actually bankrolled by McVitie's have been proved to be nothing more than slurs propagated by rival companies as the latest salvo in the escalating 'Biscuit Wars'.)

The commercial specification of the McVitie's digestive as the favourite of the British dunking public probably reflects the market and cultural dominance of that particular brand over its rivals. It is without doubt the country's leading digestive.

Having cleared up the issue of the best biscuit to dunk in a cup of tea it would be instructive for newcomers to Britain to consider the dynamics, motivations and philosophical imperatives that drives a nation to dunk in the first place.

Tea may well be the liquid refreshment that sustains this great nation of ours, but the biscuit that accompanies it is very much the icing on the cake of the drink. A cup of tea is the pause that refreshes, but the biscuit is the added treat that elevates the whole experience into one of everyday indulgence. No one ever truly *needs* the biscuit, but in our mind's eye we all *deserve* the biscuit.

To dunk the biscuit takes the whole experience on to a higher level of enjoyment. And meaning. Strip the experience to its very basics and one is inevitably faced with the realisation that what we are dealing with is a fundamental contemplation of the duality of life. In life things are described as being black or white, up or down, good or evil, left or right, positive or negative, real or imaginary, fish or chicken. The tea and the biscuit fits firmly within this dichotian analysis of our very being. The tea is wet, the biscuit is dry. But – and here is the philosophically profound core of what we are dealing with in this seemingly run-of-the-mill everyday scenario – the dunked biscuit is both wet and dry.

The dunked biscuit is nothing less than a physical attempt to reconcile the two mutually exclusive halves of our dichotomous world. Within the confines of this thin baked good what we are saying to ourselves, in a very real sense, is that diametrically opposed opposites can co-exist. Black can be white, up can be down, good can be evil, left can be right, positive can be negative, real can be imaginary, fish can be chicken, and dry can be wet.

But the metaphor of the dunked biscuit, not content with this genius-like level of meaning, goes further still.

That's because inherent in the reality of the dunked biscuit is the possibility of oblivion. Leave the biscuit too long in the tea and it will disintegrate. Worse still, immerse the biscuit just a split second beyond the optimum length of time and it will let you retrieve it from the mug, but fall apart, and into your lap, on the way to your mouth. The common British phrase may describe the discomfort and undesirability of having 'egg on your face' but the far more often experienced, and more distressing, reality is that of having 'biscuit on your trousers'.

All of which leads to the conclusion that while the French swan about in the mistaken belief that they have contributed the most to the development of philosophy in the last hundred years with the invention of existentialism – a school of thought that has it that life is, essentially, meaningless – it is in fact the British that have developed the more revolutionary, more profound, and more life-enhancing theory. At its very heart the British philosophy of Dunked Biscuitialism states nothing less than the belief that the impossible is possible, if you are willing to take the risk. And what better philosophy could there be to face the uncertainties that lie ahead for us all?

~ 43 ~

Where was the Magna Carta signed?

At the bottom.

NB: It is a worrying sign of the generally falling standards of British education that 63 per cent of school-leavers today have no idea of the historical significance of this joke, nor indeed were able to supply the punchline to it when the question was posed to them on the interactive whiteboards that every classroom now has and that have made teaching, apparently, so much better. Obviously the lack of knowledge of our nation's history is regrettable, but the lack of knowledge amongst our country's youth of our proud heritage of corny jokes is unforgivable. To rectify this shocking dereliction of duty by, ultimately, a government that once gave its priorities just before gaining office as being 'Education. Education. Education' there is given in the following question a list of five of the key corny jokes that every citizen of this land should know. That such a list should be of equal use to both newcomers to the country, and to so many of the children who were born and bred and buttered here, is a shocking indictment of things that need to be indicted shockingly.

~ 44 ~

What are the main corny old jokes that it is important for any prospective British citizen to know?

1 'My dog's got no nose.'
  'How does he smell?'
  'Terrible!'

2 'Doctor! Doctor! I think I'm a pair of curtains!'
  'Pull yourself together, man.'

3 Q. Why did the chicken cross the road?
  A. To get to the other side.

4 Q. What time did the Chinaman go to the dentist?
  A. Tooth – hurtee.

5 Q. What's brown and sounds like a bell?
  A. Dunggg!

~ 45 ~

What is 'Just Not Cricket'?

'Just not cricket' is a phrase that is dear to the heart of the British. It sums up our belief in the value of fair play. If something is 'just not cricket' then that thing has not been done fairly. Or by the rules.

This is based on the obviously dubious premise that life is, in fact, a game, and as such has rules. And if it does have rules, then clearly the fairest rules to base the rules of life on are the rules of cricket.

A very British example of the use of this phrase would be the scenario in which a hoody-ed 'yoof' pushed to the front of a bus queue and boarded the W3 you had been waiting for outside Finsbury Park tube station. In such circumstances it would be appropriate to reprimand said 'yoof' with the rebuke: 'I say old chap, that's just not cricket.' (But, for other reasons, it may not be the wisest course of action.)

For many residents of this splendid isle however, what is truly distressing is that these days cricket itself is 'just not cricket'. There are two strands to this malaise.

First there is the thought that has lurked around the nether regions of many an English cricket aficionado that for various reasons, and by various means, those jolly old foreigners that we taught the game to don't play it properly. For example, for a long time the all-conquering West Indian test team weren't really 'playing the game' by having lots of really good fast bowlers that they would insist on picking, all together, for every game. Then there are the Pakistanis who (allegedly) sometimes indulge in the odd spot of ball tampering, the Sri Lankans, whose best bowler actually doesn't bowl the ball, but chucks it, the Australians, who relentlessly wear down our plucky lads by calling them names, the South Africans, whose very captain admitted to match fixing, and the Indians who sabotage touring teams by offering them dodgy Indian food. Only New Zealand seem to remain with their reputation relatively intact.

All this seems to ignore the fact that it was an English team touring Australia in the 1930s that bowled the first bouncer, as it were, in this long innings of dodgy cricketing practices, when the captain, Jardine, instructed his bowlers to bowl not at the stumps, but at the Australian players' bodies. At the time it was an outrage that rocked the world of sport. But seeing as fifty years later the Australians sent *Neighbours* over to these shores, the pain and damage inflicted by one country on another has probably been evened out.

The other reason that cricket is 'just not cricket' any more is that the game itself has changed. Traditionally county cricket games lasted three days, while Test matches between countries lasted five days. Then, as interest and attendances fell, one-day cricket was invented. In this form of the game a match was reduced to a single innings for each side and so could be completed in one day. This was termed 'limited over' cricket. England have further refined this idea by creating the idea of 'limited talent' cricket in which a putative one-day international can be completed in far less time than one day. Obviously this fits in supremely well with the busy lives of most people in Britain today. However, in order to truly maximise the viewing potential for cricket in this country the powers that be are working on a version of the game that can be played out in the half-time interval during TV coverage of a Premiership football match.

Given all this, the continued usage of the phrase 'it's just not cricket' is a reassurance that some things in this country remain untainted by 'progress'.

NB: Though the phrase 'it's just not cricket' would undoubtedly be understood in Wales, Scotland and Northern Ireland, it would be politic, in order not to offend nationalistic feelings, to substitute the word 'cricket' with 'rugby', 'caber-tossing' and 'the marching season' as appropriate.

~ 46 ~

*Can you name all the actors
who played Doctor Who in the
Wilderness Years between Tom Baker
and Christopher Ecclestone?*

Peter Davison
Colin Baker
Sylvester McCoy
Paul McGann
George Lazenby

~ 47 ~

How should every Briton behave on the first really hot, sunny day of the year?

You should smile at everyone. Be happy. Walk to work with a spring in your step and joy in your heart admiring, as you go, the birds singing in the trees, the sun-dappled flowers drowsily nodding hello from every front garden, and the happy, laughing children skipping to school without a care in the world.

On the second day you must return to your normal, grumpy, whingeing, essentially dissatisfied self.

And you must remember not to water the garden because a hosepipe ban will have just come into effect.

~ 48 ~

What is the correlation between Cliff Richard and Tim Henman?

Both Cliff Richard and Tim Henman, despite being very good at what they do, are inextricably linked by the fact they are terminally unhip.

But in this particular field of endeavour the crown undoubtedly belongs to Cliff. This is most bizarre, as he is the only British artist to have had hit single records in six separate decades. Even more remarkable, and more rare, than Cliff's success over six decades is the fact that, apart from a brief period at the start of his career, he has been continuously unfashionable for five decades.

From the Swinging Sixties, right through to our current Arctic Manque decade, the so-called cogniscenti have sneered every time a Cliff song has serenaded the airwaves. But in that time he has seen off, amongst others, Merseybeat, psychedelia, prog rock, glam rock, heavy metal, punk, new wave, new romantics, Goths, the ska revival, indie rock, rave, grunge and Brit pop. However, his unfashionability is so ingrained in the warp and weft of British cultural life that even his achievement in the year 2000 of the rock-and-roll nirvana of having a song banned from the airwaves by Radio One could do nothing to help him.

Tim Henman's great crime has been to be the best male tennis player that Britain has produced since the Second World War. On the face of it, to borrow a song title from Cliff, this should be a cause for 'Congratulations'. (And celebrations). Britain, however, is a far more complex nation than that. Of course, there are some who hold Mr Henman in great esteem. But they are far outnumbered by those who regard him with condescension, or even something akin to affronted resentment. The problem stems from the fact that while Tim Henman is very good at what he does, he is, regrettably, not as good as the very best. For some reason this has annoyed an inordinate amount of people. Further than that he has been hindered by his name.

Timothy is not the name of a sporting hero. And shortening it to Tim doesn't count as a great improvement. Both names are, in fact, comic. Hence the put-upon, forty-year-old, still living at home and under his mother's thumb, played by Ronnie Corbett in the sitcom *Sorry* was called Timothy. And Harry Enfield's gormless toff was called Tim Nice-But-Dim. So having been christened Timothy was always going to be a heavily sliced, cross-court backhand for the young lad to have to return. On top of that, he grew up with a happy childhood, loving parents, and a reasonably privileged financial background. Why this should matter is that it gave Henman an incredibly dull backstory.

But the real nail in the coffin for Henman was his personality. That's because he didn't seem to have one.

Unfortunately, in tennis, more than in any other sport played at the highest level, personality and character matter maybe even more than supreme ability. Four hours into a men's single final, when both players are on the very edge of their physical capabilities, but still pulling off shots of unbelievable skill, power or finesse, what the enthralled crowd is witnessing transcends sport. What each player is doing is questioning his opponent's very existence. Every shot is nothing less than a physical manifestation of the ultimate question 'Who are you?' Every return is the unequivocal reply 'This is who I am. Who are you?'

So even if Tim Henman had won Wimbledon, it would not have been enough for him to achieve greatness. Because he would always be who he was – a thoroughly nice young man who was very good at tennis. And in today's Britain we want more from our sporting heroes than we did in the 1950s.

But seeing as it cannot be long before Tim Henman hangs up his racquet after playing his last match, it is probably time to reveal that while he may not have won Wimbledon he did, in fact, save Britain from untimely destruction. This narrow escape from oblivion for the nation dates back to those days in Tim's career when he was hyped-up beyond belief. When he made it to the Wimbledon semi-final in 1998 the pressure truly started to build. It is a little-known fact that immediately before he went on court to play his match with Pete Sampras he was approached by a delegation of physicists and astrophysicists from Cambridge University.

With the use of diagrams, and sophisticated computer modelling, they demonstrated to Henman that, should he win the semi and make it to the Wimbledon Final, so great would be the weight of expectation focused on his shoulders by the whole nation that there was a very real danger that the pressure generated could cause Centre Court to collapse in on itself. Once that had started nothing could stop it. The black hole created by this nexus of super-concentrated expectation would possess so great a gravity field that it would continue to suck in more and more of its surroundings. The destruction would only begin to peter out as it reached the coast of France where Gallic indifference meant no one really cared whether Tim Henman won or lost. The nightmare scenario that the scientists confronted Henman with was one in which the whole of Britain was reduced down to a blob of super-dense matter roughly the size of a tennis ball, spinning in a black void of nothingness that used to be Britain.

No record was made of Tim Henman's response to this, until now, secret meeting. All that history records is that he lost his semi-final to Sampras 6-3, 4-6, 7-5, 6-3. And that he also lost three subsequent Wimbledon semi-finals. Greater love has no man than he should lay down his career for the sake of his country.

Rumour has it that the film rights to this story were bought by Steven Spielberg for a vast sum of money. Indeed the movie entitled *Henman Horizon* was all set to go into production when the star contracted to play Tim – Will Smith – suffered a freak accident while shopping for baked beans at the Rodeo Drive branch of Budgens.

~ 49 ~

Can you match the following regional cheeses with the outline of their county of origin?

A.   Wensleydale
B.   Lancashire
C.   Single Gloucester
D.   Yarg
E.   Shropshire Blue

Answer: A2, B1, C4, D3, E5

~ 50 ~

What is the correct response when confronted on the street by a charity mugger, a.k.a. a chugger?

The correct response is 'I'm sorry, I haven't got time to talk to you right now.' Obviously this is code. Because, in reality, you probably have got time to talk to the chugger, you just don't want to. Say 'I'm sorry, I haven't got time to talk to you right now' and, by law, the chugger has to let you go on your way. What is not so well-known is that if the chugger persists in trying to continue the exchange by saying 'But this will only take a minute...', you are perfectly within your rights to hit them. Thankfully very few people take up this right, but it does exist. It is known in legal circles as 'Prescott's Law'.

Also what very few people don't realise is that the chuggers don't actually work for the charity. They work for companies who act as professional fund-raisers for the charity. In return for a surprisingly large proportion of the first year's donations that you sign up for, these companies provide the charities with standing orders that will, the charities hope, create an ongoing income flow greater than their initial cost. Practically this makes a lot of sense.

Morally, however, the water is somewhat cloudier. After all, being accosted in the street in order to raise money for people worse off than yourself plays on two complex emotions. First the chugger hopes to elicit feelings in you of sympathy. Being sympathetic is undoubtedly an admirable characteristic. However, the second emotion involved is not so altruistic. It's guilt. Walk away from an exchange whose key thrust is 'surely you can afford to contribute the cost of your daily cappuccino to alleviate the suffering of these poor, blighted souls' and only the most cold-hearted of bastards wouldn't feel a twinge of guilt. Being made to feel guilty as you walk down the street is bad enough, but when you consider that someone, somewhere, is making a no doubt very reasonable living from doing this, and it all becomes even more uncomfortable.

Which isn't to say the people of Britain aren't, naturally, charitable and sympathetic to the plight of others. Because we are. You just have to look to the spontaneous response to the Boxing Day tsunami to see that. Or Live Aid. Or Comic Relief. It's just that, maybe, we don't want to face a hard sell that requires you sign up on the spot every time we walk down the street. It would be objectionable if it was double glazing that was being sold. But when it's a charity, with its implications of guilt and redemption, maybe it's worse. Especially if someone, somewhere, is making money from it.

All of which brings us back to a key facet of the British psyche that any incomer would do well to understand. On the whole, the British don't like to make a fuss. That's why 'I'm sorry, I haven't got the time' is such a useful, and essentially British, phrase.

~ 51 ~

Are the lives of architects and designers as relentlessly well-organised and tasteful as their homes that are endlessly featured in the Sunday supplement magazines?

No.

~ 52 ~

How far did Eddie
'The Eagle' Edwards fly?

73.5 metres.

But obviously there's more to it than that.

In the 1988 Winter Olympics held at Calgary in Canada, Michael 'Eddie The Eagle' Edwards, an extremely long-sighted plasterer from the notoriously unmountainous town of Cheltenham in Gloucestershire, was Great Britain's only entrant in both the 70m and 90m ski jumping competition.

He wasn't very good. But not being very good didn't stop him from being the best ski jumper in Britain. The fact that there weren't any other ski jumpers in Britain does cast his premier national status in a somewhat different light, but we're not here to quibble over such trifling details. After all, the fact that there weren't any ski jumps to practise on in Britain did mean that ski jumping was very unlikely to seriously threaten football as the nation's favourite sport.

That Eddie had made it to Calgary at all was a triumph in itself. Even more so when you realise he'd only been practising the sport for two years. And before arriving in America he'd never actually jumped on snow. On top of all that, when he went out in the cold his milk-bottle thick glasses did have a tendency to fog up.

What's more, he was also twenty pounds heavier than the next heaviest competitor. Which, when you're trying to soar through the air like a bird, must be a little bit of a handicap.

It's hardly surprising, then, that he finished in last place in both jumps. What is surprising, however, is that he became a true, British Olympic hero. So while Sir Steve Redgrave may have achieved iconic sporting status by winning rowing gold medals in seventeen Olympic games in succession or whatever his frankly unnecessarily excessive record was, Eddie the Eagle did much the same by failing abjectly in one single games.

That's why he is the one, essential, British Olympian. Because we British love a failure. Just as long as the failure tries his best. And loses with a smile on his face. Which is exactly what Eddie 'The Eagle' Edwards did. In so doing he put a smile on the face of a nation that, in truth, rarely takes winners to its heart. Unless, of course, you're Red Rum.

The fact that Eddie actually was a success in that his jump of 73.5 metres was the British record, is largely forgotten. And rightly so.

What's also forgotten is that in light of the coverage Eddie got for not being very good, the International Olympic Committee changed the rules so that, in order to be allowed to compete in an Olympic Games, competitors had to have finished in the top half of at least one international competition.

Which only goes to show that the people who run the Olympics are a bunch of humourless bastards with no sense of fun.

On his return to Cheltenham Eddie was accorded the decidedly British accolade of a non-victory procession around the town. And three years later he released a single *Mun Nimeni On Eetu** which soared to the number two slot in the Finnish hit parade.

That his magic reached beyond the shores of a nation that cherishes failure can also be gauged by the fact that during the 1988 closing ceremony the President of the Games summed up events like this:

> '...at this Olympic Games some competitors have
> won gold, and some have broken records, and one
> has even flown like an eagle...'

At which point the assembled thousands in the arena united in one voice and chanted:

> 'Eddie! Eddie! Eddie!'

So, while in absolute terms Eddie 'The Eagle' Edwards

---

* 'My Name Is Eddie'.

may only have flown 73.5 metres, by the time his skis touched down on his last jump he had travelled a far, far greater distance. He had, in fact, flown into the hearts of all the rest of us ordinary people who are never going to be very good at anything, but who were touched by the genius of a man who had a dream and had a go.

Which, when you think about it, is an achievement very few sportsmen have ever matched.

~ 53 ~

Why does Britain have a Royal Society for the Prevention of Cruelty to Animals, but only a National Society for the Prevention of Cruelty to Children?

The only logical explanation is that in Britain animals are more important than children to the Royal Family.

~ 54 ~

Chips or fries?

Chips. Every time. Chips are genuinely, gloriously, full-bodiedly British. Fries, on the other hand, are a preposterous American imposition on that most noble of vegetables – the potato. They are the annoyingly stick-thin super-model of the spud-based snack world, and as such should be universally shunned by all Britons of good taste as being the depressing, over-hyped fashion victims they truly are. A fry is nothing more than a chip with anorexia. A chip in denial of its true nature. A chip who ridiculously believes that if only it could hang out in *Baywatch*, or *Beverly Hills 90210*, or with the sun-drenched 'beautiful people' of *The OC*, everything would 'magically' be so much better.

But who, exactly, is kidding who?

A single fry is in no way a satisfying mouthful. Indeed you need to combine a whole bunch of them together just to get somewhere near a mouthful, whereas a single chip is something you can really get your teeth into. A single chip speaks of a hard-working integrity and simple wholesomeness that a single fry wouldn't recognise if it knocked on its door late at night and asked to come in for a cup of tea.

It's like the difference between mushy peas and guacamole.

On top of all that, even the very name of 'fries' is ridiculous. That's because it's short for 'french fries', a name brought back to the United States from Europe by returning GIs after the Second World War. But, as anyone with even a passing knowledge of continental cuisine will realise, France isn't big on eating 'fries'. That honour actually falls to Belgium. So the Americans named their favourite food after completely the wrong country.

Throw in the fact that a fry has a far higher fat-absorbing surface area to volume ratio than the humble chip and you realise that not only are chips aesthetically, historically, and culturally better for you, they are also far healthier for you than a fry.

And another thing. You would sound a right pillock if you were to say to your mates after a night out on the tiles that maybe you should stop for something to eat at the 'Fry Shop'.

~ 55 ~

*Why is the new law that prevents
'demonstrations' within a specified
distance of the British Parliament
fundamentally un-British?*

Britain has a long and proud history of freedom of speech.
It is one of the traditions that makes Britain Britain.

Right the way back to the Magna Carta, which
sought to limit the powers the king held over his people,
the idea that the citizens of this land had rights that could
not be taken away from them was a fundamental cornerstone in the forging of our nation. Freedom of speech has
long been one of those rights. But it is a right that was
only earned after a long struggle. The struggle probably
truly began after the invention and spread of the printing
press had made it easy for views to be expressed and
circulated. The response by the Crown was to introduce
pre-publication licensing laws.

Later the Levellers opposed Charles the First, and
then the dictator Cromwell (whom they originally helped
to gain power) on the grounds that both were contraven-
ing the rights of citizens, including the right to free

A democrat

speech. Later still the philosopher John Stuart Mill defended freedom of speech on the basis that it is only by allowing beliefs to be criticised that we can be justified in believing that they are true.

Just over two hundred years ago, in the 1790s, following the order threatening the execution of Louis XVI during the French Revolution, the British Prime Minister introduced a number of laws that what would no doubt today be dubbed 'anti-terror measures' including sedition laws and the suspension of *habeas corpus*. But the Whig politician Charles James Fox, knowing that free speech was a cause worth fighting for, stood up in Parliament and declared:

> 'All the true constitutional watchfulness of England was dead to the real danger...we are come to the moment when the question is, whether we shall give to the King, that is the executive government, complete power over our thoughts.'

Today the importance of the British tradition of free speech has probably been best summed up in a 2006 article written by the philosopher AC Grayling entitled 'The Case For Freedom':

> 'Without free speech, people cannot receive and impart information, debate matters of fact and opinion, take an informed part in politics, hold public officials to account, assert their rights and defend their interests, and speak up in the interest of others whose case they care about. There can be no democracy without it. It underwrites the possibility of a free press and independent legal institutions. Without free speech this entire apparatus fails; and any interference with it or

diminuation of it constitutes a threat to all other freedoms and rights.'

Impassioned and important though Mr Grayling's arguments are, they do not address the real reason why the law banning demonstrations within a specified distance of Parliament is fundamentally, and demonstrably, un-British.

That reason is this. The specified distance within which demonstrations are banned is given as one kilometre.

One kilometre!

This is Britain, we measure distances in miles.

That's why every true patriot must oppose this law. Or at the very least fight to get it amended.

~ 56 ~

*Which of the following are early
kings of Britain and which are
items of furniture available at the
Edmonton branch of IKEA?*

Hensvik
Edred
Fridolf
Edwy
Arild
Svein
Edefors
Athelstan
Knut
Ivar

Answer: Edefors, Ivar, Arild, Hensvik and Fridolf are all available at
Ikea. (If you're willing to queue at the checkouts).

~ 57 ~

Where is the best place in Britain to go for free, existential, advice?

The best place to go is Embankment tube station on the Northern line of London's Underground system. You can be either on a train, or on the platform. But you need to be in position when the train pulls to a halt and the doors of the carriage open. Then you will hear the following elegant, profound, and eternally relevant, advice:

'Mind The Gap. Mind The Gap.'

London Underground levies no charge for these words of wisdom.

~ 58 ~

If you had to describe the English language in culinary terms which dish would best represent it?

Many learned people have pondered long and hard on this question. Though it can still be the subject of heated debate around closing time in pubs and clubs across the land, the general consensus seems to be that if you did have to describe the English language in culinary terms the dish which would best represent it would be a stew.

Contrast this with culinary analogies of other languages and this may seem, at first, to be a somewhat demeaning description. After all French, with its elegance, precision and codified disdain, is clearly haute cuisine. And Italian, which loops and swirls splashing its meaning round the edge of your mouth and over that white shirt you foolishly chose to wear, is equally clearly a bowl of spaghetti smothered in rich, delicious, decidedly more-ish sauce. But then again, at least a stew isn't the functional efficiency of the bratwurst and sauerkraut that represents the German language and that fills you up and keeps you going, but doesn't exactly leave you gagging for your next meal.

However, such a comparison demeans the true, subtly glorious, nature of a stew. A stew is warming, and wholesome, and hearty. And its constituent parts are unified by a gravy so delicious that once you've finished your meal you can't resist mopping up your plate with a piece of bread. What's more, if the stew has been simmering for long enough it will be replete with vaguely recognisable chunks of food, whose original nature has long since melded into the gravy, enriching its flavours, yet somehow, texturally, contrasting it.

If, as an aspiring Briton, this seems an analogy that is somewhat hard to grasp, then the following practical exercise may be of use. Below is listed a list of phrases in common use in Britain today that may, at first, be hard to understand. Anyone seeking to successfully integrate into British life should know how they are used and what they mean. Knowing where the phrases originate gives some idea of how the depth of flavour in the English language reflects the complexity of the nation that speaks it.

A COCK AND BULL STORY

This is a story that is a load of made-up nonsense. It derives from the eighteenth century when travel around Britain was conducted via coaches. Equidistant between London and Birmingham, and between Oxford and Cambridge, was the Buckinghamshire town of Stony Stratford. Naturally the town became a wayside stop for all kinds of travellers and commerce. The two main

A cock and a bull

coaching inns of the town were The Cock and The Bull. These hostelries soon started to vie with each other to see who could produce the most exciting travellers' tales for circulation round the country. They were tales whose often unreliable and exaggerated nature soon led to them being denigrated as 'Cock and Bull' tales.

The dismissive phrase can even be shortened to just 'cock', and may well be the root of spoken rubbish being described as 'bullshit'.

EGG ON

This means to encourage someone to do something. Its roots can be found in the Anglo-Saxon *eggian*, meaning to spur on.

FREEZE THE BALLS OFF A BRASS MONKEY

When weather is particularly cold it can be described as being 'cold enough to freeze the balls off a brass

monkey'. It is a decidedly odd turn of phrase that, thankfully, has nothing to do with real monkeys or the temper-
ature of their gonads. It is, in fact, an old nautical term.
On board the men-of-war ships of the eighteenth
century, the young boys who were small enough to
squeeze up to the barrels of the cannons and prime them
with gunpowder were called 'powder monkeys'. The iron
cannonballs themselves were stacked up in pyramids in a
tray that had small circular indentations in them. The
trays were made of brass so that the balls would neither
stick to them nor rust. Hence the trays were called 'brass
monkeys'. But in cold weather brass contracts faster than
iron. And if it was cold enough the brass indentations
would contract so much that the balls would fall out.
Hence the term.

HOBNOB
To hobnob with someone means to socialise with that
person. It is a term that is often used with a derogatory
implication of snobbish exclusivity on the parts of both
the hobnobber and the hobnobbee. It is a relatively
modern term that derives from the all-too-common practice of getting your favourite biscuits out only when
people you really like come round.

GONE FOR A BURTON
Something, or someone, that's Gone For A Burton, is
something or someone that has suffered a mishap or has

disappeared. It is a phrase that derives from an advertising slogan. The advertisement in question was for Burton's Ales and ran before the Second World War. In the ad a football team is shown with one player missing. The headline explains that the player has 'Gone For A Burton'.

During the Second World War members of the RAF, with a decidedly black sense of humour, purloined the phrase for any pilot who crashed into the sea. The sea, incidentally, was commonly referred to by the RAF at the time as 'the drink'.

THAT OLD CHESTNUT

This applies to a joke, reason or excuse that has been heard loads of times before. Its origins lie in an 1816 play by William Diamond called *The Broken Sword*. In the play Captain Xavier constantly repeats a joke about a cork tree. But late on another character interrupts with the correction *'It's a chestnut. I've heard you tell the joke twenty-seven times and it's a chestnut.'* Some time later William Warren, an American actor who had been playing the part of Captain Xavier interrupted a guest at a society dinner who had launched into an old joke with the put-down *'It's an old chestnut, that's what it is!'* The assembled company fell about laughing. The incident was much repeated and the phrase eventually came into common usage.

AS BOLD AS BRASS

This phrase refers to someone who does something blatantly with no fear of the consequences. It dates back to the 1770s when it was against the law for information on Parliament to be published. One London printer, however, did just that. He was arrested and brought before the local magistrate Brass Crosby. Brass Crosby let the printer off. Then he himself was arrested and ended up in jail. The public, however, were on Crosby's side and the outcry was so great that he was soon released. And before long his name entered the English language in a phrase that originally described someone with the courage of their convictions and who was unafraid to act.

~ 59 ~

If, as Sir Elton John states,
'Sorry Seems To Be The Hardest Word'
why do train operating companies
apologise so frequently for the late
running of their services?

Because they don't really mean it.

~ 60 ~

Who is more British — the Briton who actually lives, and pays their taxes, in Britain, or the ex-patriot Brit who has moved abroad?

Somewhat surprisingly it is the ex-patriot Brit who has moved abroad. That is because having moved abroad they realise how important it is to maintain their cultural identity. And, indeed, to celebrate it. What complicates the matter is that they also have to justify their decision to leave the land that created that cultural identity.

The easiest way to do this is to argue that their home-land is changing. And the easiest way to do this is to highlight the influx of foreigners who arrive unable to speak the language, set themselves up in almost exclusively foreign enclaves, and insist on maintaining their cultural identity. And, indeed, celebrating it.

~ 61 ~

Are people under the age of sixty allowed to play bowls?

Legally there are no restrictions on the age of bowls players. However, tradition says otherwise. Which is why any bowling green is usually the exclusive playground of the elders of society. A few years back an outrageously gifted bowls player of very tender years did emerge. Unfortunately, this veritable Cristiano Ronaldo of the slender creeping red fescue sward was also encumbered with a temperament that nodded vigorously towards Mr George Best. Consequently after a series of misdemeanours, he was banned from the sport. For life.

Behind the specific charges of his banishment lay a deeper, problematic, subtext. He was just too young. The whole story was immortalised in celluloid in the exceedingly British sporting movie *Balls Of Fire* starring the actor Paul Kaye. For some reason the film didn't really crack America.

That the iron fist of the powers that be in the seemingly genteel world of bowls could crush the youthful butterfly of talent in its grasp reflects a little-known truth that lies at the heart of the sport. While Southampton boasts a bowls green that dates back to 1187, and Lewes in Sussex claims a green laid in the grounds of its castle just after the Norman conquest, the history of the sport predates both by a considerable amount.

The surprising truth is that the sport of bowls dates back to Iron Age Britain. This revelation was first revealed with the advent of aerial photography. It was thanks to this god-like perspective that the true significance of a site such as Maiden Castle in Dorset became clear. The centre of the site is a relatively flat area of grass. Surrounding it is a series of ditches. Other sites across the ancient landscape of Britain boast similar features. Often the series of ditches is replaced by a single continuous trench. The similarities of the topography of these sites to present-day bowls greens is unmistakeable. Obviously over the years their irregular shapes have been formalised into a rectangle or square. (Some scholars think this may have been an imposition of the Normans.)

As for the purpose of these sites, it is only through the relatively recent unearthing of a shard of Iron Age macrame that the truth has been revealed. And, by way of warning, if you are at all squeamish it's best you look away now.

The raised, entrenched sites, often described as forts, were in fact ritualised playing fields. When the young men of one tribe went to war with their neighbours, the elders of the tribe would wait on these fields for their return. If victorious, the marauding youth would triumphantly dump the spoils of their victory at the feet of their elders. Most prized among the booty would be the severed heads of the enemies that they had slain. The elders of the tribe would then compound the defeat and disgrace of their foes by using the heads for a game that would still be recognisable today as a decidedly grisly form of bowls.

But if the heads were the 'bowls', then what were the 'jacks'? Well let's just say that originally the game was played with two 'jacks' and they weren't completely spherical. And scholars also believe that there is considerable significance in the earliest written reference to the game in which it is called 'bawls'.

It has been argued that these ancient sites are far too big to successfully play any such game upon. But after much debate scholars have concluded that these sites weren't just built to play the game. They were also built to intimidate the enemies of the tribe. The subliminal message being that if a tribe needs so huge a playing area they clearly sever a lot of heads each time they wage war. They were, in effect, the Wembley stadiums of ancient Britain.

That such a bloodthirsty history can lie behind the soporific sight of elderly men and women rolling composite plastic balls across a close-cropped lawn on a summer's afternoon just highlights the truth that behind this ancient land of ours there is often much more going on than meets the eye.

~ 62 ~

What cut of meat has been ennobled with a knighthood?

Back in the sixteenth century, King Henry the Eighth was so taken with a roast loin of beef he was eating that he reached for his sword and dubbed it 'sir' loin. The tradition of giving honours to cuts of meat favoured by the royal family has continued down the years, though the recent elevation of Lord Turkey Twizzler and Dame Doner Kebab have lead critics to suggest that attempts by the House of Windsor to find the 'common touch' have gone a little too far.

~ 63 ~

Does the person you are calling really know you are waiting?

No.

They know that someone is waiting. It might be you, it might be someone else. So when your telephone call to whoever you have called can't be connected because that person is already on another call and you receive the automated message that 'the person you are calling knows you are waiting' it is not the whole picture. However, it would be a harsh critic indeed that would call the message an outright lie. It is more a case of misinformation that, on the face of it, is supposed to be reassuring, but when you delve into the reality of the situation, covers up a different state of affairs.

The point of the message is that it is designed to keep you on the line. And all the time you are on the line you are racking up call charges. In effect you are paying to wait. Now whereas it is true that the British love to queue, this manifestation of the practice is probably a step too far.

It is also worth considering the psychological impact of being made to wait in this fashion. Surely if the person you are calling knows *you* are waiting but still refuses to end the call they are already on then, obviously, they think that the person they are already talking to is more important than you. It's far more worthwhile to natter on to that other person about, for all you know, matters as inconsequential as the latest BOGOF offers at Kwik Save or Dr Legg's surprise return to *EastEnders*, than it is to talk to you.

No wonder that those nine simple, seemingly innocent, words have the effect of surreptitiously chipping away at your already endangered self-esteem.

But step back from your position as victim in this telephonic scam and consider it from the position of victee and are things really any better?

The only information the person you are calling receives is an annoying beeping noise interrupting their ongoing call. Admittedly this can prove useful as, should it be needed, it gives them an excuse to terminate the existing call they may be desperate to finish.

But if they don't want to finish the existing call they are faced with an unenviable dilemma. Could the call on hold be something really important? Or is it slightly less important than the call they are already involved in? And if, in an endeavour to resolve the dilemma they attempt to juggle between the calls in the way the phone manual assures you is really easy, will they actually cut one, or even both, of the callers off the line like they did the last time they tried to 'manage' their calls.

And, bloody hell, wasn't it a whole lot simpler when, if you were on the phone and someone rang, they got an engaged tone and just had to try ringing back later?

All of which may well lead you to ponder on the origin of the term 'phoney'. It came into usage in the years after the telephone became a common household object. And it was a term that sought to describe how the human voice sounded not quite real. That it sounded, somehow, fake. And it is a description that may well be worth resurrecting as the plethora of telephone services, tariffs and increasingly 'sophisticated' mobile phones in Britain today try to convince you they are inexorably making your life better.

So, does the person you are calling know you are waiting?

No. It's just another phoney claim.

~ 64 ~

Which is more important, custard or gravy?

One is sweet, one is savoury. One is light, one is dark. One is ying, one is yang.

But Britain fuels itself with both. To imagine a land where only one held sway is to imagine a land very different from the one in which we live.

If you like, custard and gravy are the two sides of our nation's split personality. Custard is the side that speaks of fun, enjoyment, even silliness. Gravy is the world of work, of duty, of seriousness. Each contrasts the other, yet each balances the other.

That's why the ideal British meal would feature both custard *and* gravy. (Though obviously not on the same plate*.) And the ideal British life would do just the same.

And in life, just as at dinner time, both the custard and gravy should be free of lumps.

All of which sheds an entirely new, philosophically profound, light on the perennial question posed by

---

* Unless, of course, you're eating at Heston Blumenthal's new flagship restaurant *Cauldron Bubble*.

generation after generation of British mothers as they fuss over their families:

'Shall I make more gravy/custard?'

Yes, it is essentially a question about food. But in truth it is a question about so much more.

~ 65 ~

What is the correct way to pronounce the word 'bath'?

This is a far more complex question than it first seems, as the answer depends on where you are. If you are south of a line bisecting the country from west to east running through a point just south of Birmingham, you say 'bahth'. However this only applies if you are east of a line that runs from Cheltenham through Bristol and Bath (the town) and on to the south coast. If you are west of this line you should really say 'baath'. Then again if you are north of that west-east bisector running through a point just south of Birmingham previously mentioned then the correct way to pronounce 'bath' is 'bath' with a short 'a'. If you are in any doubt as to what to do it's probably best to consult the Curator of English Language Dialects and Accents at the British Museum.

However, if this is still all too confusing your best bet is to have a shower installed instead.

~ 66 ~

Why couldn't the Daleks conquer the universe?

Conventional wisdom would have it that the Daleks couldn't conquer the universe because they couldn't go up stairs. Even though this glaring flaw in Dalek design was never taken advantage of by a succession of Dr Whos, it was their undoubted Achilles Heel. Or perhaps that should be their Achilles Wheel. So all anyone had to do . to escape from the threat of being 'Exterminate!'-d was to leg it up the nearest flight of stairs and hide in the bedroom. Luckily for the Daleks of yore, and their universe-conquering plans, they never seemed to operate in staircase-rich environments. They would ply their trade in flat-floored rooms and long corridors and remarkably pebble-free gravel pits. It is also fortunate that both spaceships and space stations eschew the use of stairs in their layouts and tend to favour lifts.

Interestingly, especially as the early 1970s were a veritable Golden Age for the Daleks, no record exists of how they would have coped in a room that had a particularly luxurious shag-pile carpet.

A dilemma

Given all this, if you did happen to be threatened by a Dalek in the 1970s while at home, probably the least safe place would have been the downstairs loo, or the kitchen, where the chances are the floor would have been covered with tiles or lino. In light of the possible deterrent effect of quite a deep carpet, the common defensive posture of hiding behind the sofa in the living room may not have been quite as silly a response as first may seem.

The latest incarnation of the Daleks, however, rectifies their well-documented shortcoming by giving them the ability to fly. Why the Daleks never thought of this before is a mystery. Especially as they were created by the individual generally thought of in Britain as being the evil genius's evil genius: Davros. Obviously, now that they can fly they stand a far greater chance of conquering the universe. Indeed, given the amount of merchandise now available in almost every retail outlet in the country, they seem well on the way to succeeding in their plan – in an economic sense at the very least.

Unfortunately, while the BBC's decision to give the Daleks the power of flight might seem like a major step forward it is, in fact, a vastly retrograde move. And a discriminatory one that a publicly funded body like the BBC should not be allowed to get away with.

To understand why this is the case we need to return to the original question.

Why couldn't the Daleks conquer the universe?

Well, the truth is, it's because they weren't supposed to be able to. That's because Davros, far from being an evil genius, was in fact a humanitarian warrior. For those who have no idea of the achievement of the man it's probably best to create a brief pen portrait of him. Certainly he was no oil painting. Not unless that oil painting had been painted by Francis Bacon and then carelessly left on top of a sunbed set to maximum for two to three days. What's more, the only part of his body he could move was one, claw-like, hand. And to get around, the bottom half of his body was encased in what was, in effect, a futuristic wheelchair.

And there you have the gist of his problems and the

starting point of the universe-wide outrage he sought to confront. To sum it all up, Davros created the Daleks to highlight the appalling problems of disabled access that existed in the past, present and future. Lesser individuals would probably have tackled the problem by writing letters to an MP, or contriving some publicity friendly stunt designed to embarrass the powers that be.

But Davros was a genius. And geniuses think of things at which we lesser mortals can only marvel. To Davros, what better way could there be to highlight the plight of the wheelchair-bound than to create a race of super-intelligent, omni-powerful beings, who should, by rights, be ruling the universe, but aren't because they can't go up stairs.

Given all this the BBC's decision to grant Daleks the power to fly is nothing but a slap in the face for a group of people in no real position to stand up and fight back. So maybe we shouldn't let the Daleks fly until the people they were created to represent have the chance to do the same.

~ 67 ~

How does someone become a 'National Treasure'?

Somewhat surprisingly there is no formalised mechanism by which this highly sought-after accolade is awarded. 'National Treasure' status seems to be solely the ad hoc gift of journalists writing newspaper and magazine articles. Confronted by, for example, the problem of writing an introduction to a piece on Alan Bennett, they will mention by way of shorthanding his cultural status and significance, that he is a 'National Treasure'. While this may well reflect the great esteem in which Mr Bennett is held by the nation, the very fact that it is one individual, i.e. the journalist, who has specified the status, should be cause for concern.

After all, if the giving of 'National Treasure' status is in the unregulated gift of journalists then surely the system is open to abuse? For example, why is it that those who are 'National Treasures' predominantly seem to come from the luvvied-up worlds of the arts and entertainment? Of course, there may well be nothing remiss in this state of affairs but until the matter is put on to some kind of ethical, formalised, and transparent footing, then it is inevitable suspicions will remain.

While this whole issue of the dishing out of 'National Treasure' status is an undoubted cause for concern in Britain, it is, in the grand scheme of things, a matter of no real importance. Being elevated to a 'National Treasure' may afford the person so honoured a warm glow of satisfaction at their breakfast table, but doesn't really enable them to lord it over their peers or the general public. And as Britain is a sophisticated, modern, meritocratic democracy it's not as if positions of real power, privilege or even legislative authority would ever be dished out in such a cavalier and morally suspect fashion.

~ 68 ~

What does many a mickle make?

A muckle.

~ 69 ~

What is the vital ingredient of all classic British Christmas songs?

Sadness.

The sadness can take many forms. It might be wistfulness, melancholy, regret or heartache, but it is always there. The following is a list of the key British Christmas songs and all of them contain emotional content that seems, on the face of it, at odds with the sentiments of the season.

'A Spaceman Came Travelling' by Greg Lake
'Last Christmas' by Wham!
'Imagine' by John Lennon
'Stop The Cavalry' by Jona Lewie
'Lonely This Christmas' by Mud
'The Power Of Love' by Frankie Goes To
    Hollywood
'Fairytale Of New York' by Shane MacGowan and
    Kirsty MacColl
'Do They Know It's Christmas?' by Band Aid

Why Britons should be repeatedly drawn to songs that act as a counterpoint to the season of joy and goodwill is yet another example of the innate good sense of the nation. Yes, of course we enjoy the celebrations Christmas brings, but deep in our very being we know that every silver lining has a cloud. Also, as the forces of commercialism guide us inexorably towards a feast of over-consumption, there is in the back of our minds a small voice that cries out 'now just hold on a minute!' It is to this voice these songs speak. So while the TV, newspapers and billboards bombard us with all the things we could gain this Christmas, the songs Britain takes to its heart during the festive season are, to a large extent, a meditation on things we have lost.

Given this analysis, Greg Lake's song becomes the key text because it beautifully describes the universal loss that means that once you pass a certain age, no matter how hard you try, you can't, metaphorically speaking, get the Christmas tree to stand up perfectly straight. That loss being, in simpler terms, a loss of innocence.

Mind you, Slade's 'So Here It Is Merry Christmas' does rather bugger up the theory. But then again it is Christmas and everyone enjoys a bit of a knees-up.

~ 70 ~

What is to blame for celebrity chefs like Gordon Ramsay and Jamie Oliver?

The blame lies way back in the late 1970s with the short-lived but deeply influential Punk Cook movement. This anti-fashion, street-led, cooking phenomena burst on to the culinary scene with a shocking manifesto best summed up in the Roneo-ed and stapled-together pages of the fanzine *Sniffing Stew*. The seminal, inarticulate article in the 'magazine' showed an illustration of three battered saucepans captioned with the now famous legend:

'This is a pan. This is another one. And this is another one. Now go cook a dish.'

Across the land a disenfranchised generation of kids disillusioned by the elaborate canoodlings of the giants of so-called Progressive Cooking saw their chance and seized it. For them, chips were no longer just going to be bought at chip shops, rather they would be made from scratch at home and displayed defiantly on their shoulders.

Stylistically the movement was fuelled at the start by Malcolm McLaren's and Vivienne Westwood's King's

Road shop *Trex*. And when the group McLaren managed, The Trex Pistols, made it to the top of the charts with the ironic anti-establishment hymn to the joys of school-dinner cabbage entitled *God Save The Greens* in the very week the nation was being force-fed the reheated Coronation Chicken of the Silver Jubilee, a corner had most definitely been turned.

Before long Punk Cook was not so much sweeping the nation as chopping, blanching and stirring it. The Hash released *White Fry-Up*. And The Buzzcook's captured the mood, and indeed the dish, of the day with *Wok Do I Get?* which started with the immortal line:

'Just want some liver like any other, wok do I get?'

Unfortunately, such a flowering of ideas and idealism soon burned itself out. But the energy and influence of such a vibrant, creative time in British cooking could never be suppressed for long. Gordon Ramsay represents the foul-mouthed aggression of the movement. And Jamie Oliver has ridden to fame and fortune by propagating the true Punk Cook spirit that anyone can do it. And do it well.

~ 71 ~

What is missing from the Union Jack?

Any reference to the nation of Wales. Mind you, it would be a tad tricky to subtly incorporate a red dragon into the design of the current flag.

~ 72 ~

What is 'forced rhubarb'?

To understand the true cultural significance of 'forced rhubarb' one must first consider the wider history of rhubarb in general, and in Britain in particular.

The first recorded use of rhubarb dates back to China almost 5,000 years ago. Rhubarb is a vegetable, but it is used as if it were a fruit. The part of the plant that is eaten is the stem. In this regard, it resembles its anaemic cousin, celery. Luckily, however, it is far more delicious to eat. But this may have something to do with the copious amounts of sugar with which it is traditionally cooked.

Rhubarb is thought to have been brought to Europe by the Italian explorer Marco Polo. In 1608 there is a recorded planting of it in Italy. By later in the seventeenth century it had made its first appearance in Britain. It was probably grown originally in Britain as a medicinal plant, but as sugar fell in price its popularity as an ingredient for puddings took off.

Unarguably the king of the rhubarb puddings is rhubarb crumble. However, in certain parts of the country small children would cut out the middle-man entirely and feast on rhubarb sticks dipped in sugar.

'Forced rhubarb' is rhubarb that has been grown in artificially created warm and dark conditions. The epicentre of the 'forced rhubarb' world is the Rhubarb Triangle of West Yorkshire that exists between the towns of Wakefield, Leeds and Morley. Legend has it that the technique for forcing rhubarb was a chance discovery made when a local farmer threw a pile of rhubarb roots on a manure heap and forgot about them. To his surprise the warmth, and the lack of light, actually encouraged accelerated growth.

Technically speaking, what he had hit upon was a biological process that scientists know as etiolation. The plants, desperately seeking light for the leaves on their crowns, grow twice as fast as normal. The result for the rhubarb consumer is a rhubarb that is sweeter and markedly less fibrous than rhubarb grown in sunlight.

In its heyday so much rhubarb was grown in the Rhubarb Triangle that daily 'Rhubarb Express' trains ran to London laden with tons of the crop. Unfortunately, one of the least examined consequences of the Second World War was the declining popularity of rhubarb. This was due to the sugar shortages that Britain endured. As a result of this a generation of children grew up associating all rhubarb-based puddings as a somewhat tart experience.

However, low-slung rhubarb forcing sheds can still be found in Yorkshire. These buildings' design has remained pretty much unchanged since they started to be built towards the end of the Victorian Age. Indeed, venture inside one and while you may well be stepping back into something from the 1880s it actually feels far more ancient. That's because, when the rhubarb is pulled, the only light allowed in the sheds comes from long, thin, taper like candles carefully placed at ten-foot intervals throughout the growing rhubarb stalks. And, as any rhubarb grower will tell you, if you still your feet, and hush your voice, and concentrate in the gloom, you will actually be able to hear the popping open of the leaves of the plant as the rhubarb grows. As the whispering rhubarb pickers bend their backs in supplication to the blessed vegetable the place resembles nothing other than a medieval cathedral, lit by the flickering candles of the faithful. If only Caravaggio had been born three hundred years later than he was, and a Yorkshireman, he would surely have put his mastery of chiaroscuro to good effect in the forcing sheds of the Rhubarb Triangle.

Luckily, these days rhubarb is enjoying something of a culinary renaissance. And the Wakefield Rhubarb Festival, held every year towards the end of January, is beginning to generate the same kind of media buzz that once surrounded Glastonbury in its early days. Unfortunately the semi-legendary commercial produced to promote the festival entitled *May the Forced be with you*, in which Luke Skywalker and Darth Vader battle it out with giant sticks of rhubarb, had to be pulled due to copyright problems.

The other type of 'forced rhubarb' to be found in contemporary Britain occurs when politicians 'answer' questions. What parallels their answers have with something that's been grown by keeping it in the dark and covering it with manure is anyone's guess. But a clue may be found in the fact that the medicinal use the ancient Chinese put rhubarb to was as a laxative.

~ 73 ~

What are the best-written lines in the whole history of British pop?

The best-written lines in the whole history of British pop appear in the 1979 Ian Dury song 'This Is What We Find'. They are as follows:

> *'Home improvement expert Harold Hill of Harold Hill*
> *Of do-it-yourself dexterity and double-glazing skill*
> *Came home to find another gentleman's kippers in the grill*
> *So he sanded off his winkle with his Black & Decker drill'*

Particular attention should be paid to the use of the word 'gentleman'.

~ 74 ~

What separates the North from the South?

The issue we are dealing with here is the oft talked-about 'North–South Divide'. Although it is frequently invoked, what it actually consists of has never been definitively defined. Some describe it in economic terms, some in sociological terms, some in political terms and some in cultural terms. Of course, it may also be a combination of some, or all, of these elements.

The gist of the economic argument is that the country is divided into two distinct zones. The South is taken to be relatively prosperous, while the North, in contrast, does not fare so well. Obviously such a macro-scale analysis is bound to include all manner of anomalies. Harrogate in Yorkshire, for example, is nothing if not a thriving, affluent area, and certain parts of London, for instance, are as run-down as the best of them. Behind the economic argument is the line of reasoning that the North prospered in the days of extractable mineral resources and heavy manufacturing industry. However the mistake was made of not diversifying when times were good so that when the resources started to run down, and manufacturing goods could be supplied far cheaper from abroad, the region entered into a period of prolonged, profound, structural decline.

Other factors that have been described in the past as highlighting the North–South Divide include house prices, earnings, government expenditure, political persuasion and, most worryingly of all, health. A recent survey, for example, has shown that Northerners eat far fewer fruit and vegetables than their southern counterparts.

Perhaps the key facet of the divide, however, is not something that can be easily pinned down and quantified. That's because the area in which the concept of the North–South Divide is strongest is in how people perceive the character of the residents of each region. The people from the North are often taken to be friendlier, and more straightforward than the unfriendly, aloof, emotionally suppressed bunch of smacked arse-faced miseries from the South who will probably shunt their aged parents into a 'home' the very first time that they get a little confused and dress the rocket and endive salad with ordinary olive oil and not the hand-pressed extra virgin that's been brought back from the annual family holiday in Tuscany.

Or to look at it all from a different angle, a very wise man once characterised the difference between the North and South in their differing responses to the slash-and-burn era-defining politics of Mrs Thatcher. The North's response was the likes of Joy Division. The

South came up with Spandau Ballet, a bunch of perfectly coiffed pretty boys who liked nothing better than to dress up as pirates.

Or, to put it in yet another light, in the North halfway through the working day they get something to eat from Greggs. In the South they have to make do with Pret a Manger.

~ 75 ~

What did Freddie Starr eat?

He ate 'my hamster'. Allegedly. The story dates back to the 13 March 1986 when the comedian Freddie Starr returned to a friend's flat late one night after a performance at a Manchester nightclub and demanded his friend's girlfriend make him a sandwich. She suggested he should make it himself. So he did. By extracting a pet hamster – named Supersonic – from a cage in the kitchen and slapping it between two slices of bread.

The end result was a sated comedian, an ex-hamster, a tearful friend's girlfriend and the legendary front page headline in the *Sun*: 'FREDDY STARR ATE MY HAMSTER'. The only fly in the ointment of the tale of the hamster in the bread was that none of it was true. But, and it is a very big but, it didn't matter. A watershed moment of popular culture in Britain had been created.

One version of the story behind the story goes like this. In 1986 zany comedian Freddie Starr, whose career wasn't exactly zenithing, had hired the PR consultant Max Clifford to promote an upcoming tour. One morning Clifford took a call from an editor of the *Sun* who, apparently, had been approached by the girlfriend of a

A sandwich unavailable at Pret A Manger

friend of Freddie Starr. Freddie and his friend had fallen out, and the friend had subsequently concocted the story about the hamster sandwich as a way of getting back at him. The editor of the paper wanted to know if they ran with the story, would Freddie resort to lawyers and seek an injunction. Clifford consulted with Starr, who wanted the story stopped. As did Starr's manager. But Max Clifford told the *Sun* editor to go ahead. As he has subsequently stated: 'I thought it was fantastic publicity. I also reckoned that most of Freddie's fans probably couldn't read or write, and the few who could wouldn't care what he ate.'

And it worked. The story was splashed all over the front page. The tour sold out. And another forty dates were added.

In his book *Read All About It*, Clifford describes the incident as the one through which he 'redefined his role in the world of PR, which later changed the industry itself'. The book then goes on to say that from that point on the very nature of PR changed – instead of him trying to persuade editors to write about his clients, they started to come to him for 'gift-wrapped stories'.

In reality what the headline embodied is that very rare beast – a win–win–win–win situation. The *Sun* sold more newspapers, Freddie Starr sold more tickets, Max Clifford made more money, and the population of Britain had a laugh on the way to work that morning. And no one got hurt. Not even Supersonic. However Max Clifford did attempt to push the story a little too far when he tried to get both Freddie and Supersonic booked on to Terry Wogan's chat show for a touching on-screen reconciliation.

Unbeknownst to Max, Supersonic had signed up to a rival PR firm and was already contracted to tour the north-west promoting a well-known chain of sandwich bars. After that the rodent decided to go it alone and cash in on his fame by opening what was supposed to be the flagship branch of his own 'Supersonic Sandwiches' franchise in Cheadle Hume. But a freak accident with a Breville sandwich toaster lead both to the demise of the venture, and Supersonic himself. The funeral was a quiet affair. Although prior commitments meant that Freddie Starr couldn't attend in person he did send a beautiful, single, red rose. In between two slices of bread.

Although what is arguably the most famous tabloid headline of all time was, in truth, little more than a bit of fun, deconstruct its meaning and there is an important lesson to be learned from it. A message that an often sceptical nation like Britain does well to keep close to its heart.

You can't believe everything that you read in the papers.

~ 76 ~

What two competing versions of British femininity are represented by Lady Di's see-through summer frock and Ginger Spice's skimpy Union Jack dress?

The two competing versions of British femininity are the lady and the ladette.

As for the item of clothing that could provide a happy meeting place for these contrasting role models, that would be a pair of Marks & Spencer's knickers.

~ 77 ~

What are the key British narratives of the moment?

Britain is a nation that defines its nature, in part, by the stories it tells itself. At any one moment in time a vast array of narratives swirl around in the collective consciousness. Some of these narratives go back centuries and are permanent fixtures. Some last for only a few months before they lose their relevance and interest and fade away for ever.

In essence, these narratives are ways of organising information. This is important as there is so much information in the world that, as individuals, we can't sensibly comprehend it all. However, organise the information into a series of narratives and we can begin to get a grip on what is going on. Or, at the very least, on what we think is going on. After all narratives are just stories, and stories aren't always true.

The narratives fall into five main categories. These are Historical, Political, Social, Economic and Cultural. For example, one of the key British Historical narratives is the story of the British Empire. And, as an example, the British Empire narrative is well worth considering as it reveals a key facet of this story-based ordering of reality. This key facet is that vastly varying versions of the same narrative can exist for different individuals or groups.

Also worth considering is the fact that the meaning of individual narratives can change over time. In the 1980s the key political narrative in Britain was Mrs Thatcher vs the Unions. But now, barely twenty years on, this almost seems like a saga from an ancient era.

Or take the endlessly revisited cultural narrative of the Swinging Sixties. Buy into this particular version of events and it seems as if everyone who lived in London was wearing psychedelic clothes, taking hallucinogenic drugs, dancing to mind-altering music, and having earth-shatteringly orgasmic guilt- and consequence-free sex every single night. But the latest estimates suggests that in 'Swinging London' there were actually only somewhere between 167 and 208 people involved in the whole 'happening scene'. Given that at the time the population of Greater London was in the region of 7,992,443 people these figures cast the Swinging Sixties narrative in a somewhat different light. However, to a large extent, the accuracy of the narrative doesn't matter. We order the world around us, and our experience of it, and indeed our reactions to it, based on what we believe the narrative to be.

All of which helps explain why one of the key political narratives preoccupying Britain at the moment – the war in Iraq – has its roots in the narratives our then

Prime Minister told to himself before he decided to get us involved.

As to the actual key British narratives of the moment these are always a matter of debate. The following list is merely our suggestion.

Political narrative: Gordon Brown's Brave New World?
Social narrative: Multi-cultural Britain
Economic narrative: Tesco/Eastern European migrants
Cultural narrative: Kate Moss and Pete Doherty

~ 78 ~

*By how much should you expect
any large-scale construction project
or computer system modernisation
scheme to go over budget?*

Anything from one hundred to three hundred per cent.

In addition, in the case of the computerisation scheme, it is reasonable to expect the new system not to work as well as the old one.

~ 79 ~

What is the most British unguent that you can spread on your toast?

Marmite.

Marmite is a sticky, shiny substance, the consistency of melted tarmac, so concentratedly dark brown it is almost black. Its flavour is salty and somewhat like fried onions, or the condensed juices scraped off the bottom of a roasting pan in which your mother has just cooked the Sunday joint of beef.

Marmite has long been a staple food of the British home. Perhaps its ultimate expression is in the form of the 'Marmite soldier', which comprises of a toasted slice of white bread that has been buttered, then thinly spread with Marmite, and finally cut into vertical strips approximately half an inch across. Ideally this should be eaten while the toast is still warm.

Few true Britons can read the above sentences without their mouths salivating and becoming gripped by an almost uncontrollable urge to go and deploy their toaster at the earliest possible opportunity. Paradoxically, however, it is also acceptably British to absolutely hate Marmite. What is definitely un-British is to be indifferent to it. If you want to truly be a part of this land of ours you need to have an opinion on it.

Indeed it is a little-known fact that at busy times at our ports and airports in the late 1990s, immigration officials were given the power to speed-process waiting queues by walking up and down them posing the one word question 'Marmite?' Anyone who greeted the query with a blank stare was then channelled off into a separate queue where a more detailed consideration of their travel documents and credentials were carried out.

What is decidedly odd is that such a cornerstone of Britain's Britishness owes its existence to a German. That's because it was Liebig, a German scientist, who was, to slightly misquote the late Bobby Pickett, 'working in his lab late one night' when he discovered that brewer's yeast could be concentrated, bottled and eaten.

By the start of the 1900s this information had made its way to Burton-on-Trent in Staffordshire, where the yeast used was a by-product of the fermentation of British beer. The Marmite Food Co, founded in 1902, developed a system in which the yeast was taken from the brewing process, then placed in tanks allowing autolysis to occur. This involves the yeast breaking down and releasing its nutrients – soluble amino acids and proteins – into a liquid suspension. The fluid is then centrifuged, concentrated and filtered several times to remove the unwanted cell walls. Then it is condensed, under vacuum conditions, until the right consistency is achieved. Finally it is blended and flavoured with vegetable extracts and spices.

All of this makes it sound as if making Marmite owes less to cooking and more to chemistry. In truth the process owes more to a far older, and more mystical, tradition. That's because what we are dealing with here is alchemy. The alchemist's dream was to take a base material and transform it into gold. But what was an unachievable fantasy for the medieval mystics, became a reality for the wizards at the Marmite Food Co. They took an unwanted waste product of brewing and turned it into black gold. Liquid black gold. Liquid black gold that you could spread on toast.

Before Marmite could achieve the fame and fortune it so richly deserved science, once more, had to step in and lend a helping Bunsen burner. The difficulty was that when Marmite first hit the streets (as it were) the great British public weren't exactly bowled over by the stuff. However, in 1912, the biochemists Hopkins and Funk proposed the theory that certain diseases might be caused by a dietary deficiency of certain vitamins. Marmite was known by its manufacturers to be rich in vitamins. Despite the infancy of the scientific theory it soon gained credibility amongst the medical fraternity of the day. The clever people who made Marmite saw their chance. Before long the sticky, brown-black spread was spreading through hospitals and schools like a knife through butter.

By the time of the First World War Marmite was included in soldiers' ration packs. It also did sterling service in the Second World War where it was supplied to military personnel in prisoner-of-war camps. And, just as the British housewife was urged to 'Dig For Victory' to contribute to the war effort to defeat Hitler and the gathering forces of international fascism, she was also patriotically asked, Marmite-wise, to 'use it sparingly just now'.

Some idea of just how deeply ingrained Marmite has become in the national psyche in the years that followed can perhaps be gauged by an incident that occurred high in the mountains of India in 1994. It was there that a British backpacker was kidnapped and held hostage by Kashmiri separatist rebels. Thankfully, he was eventually released and arrived back home in Britain. Apparently one of the first things he did when he made it back to the bosom of his mightily relieved family was to eat some Marmite on toast. A feast that he described at the time like this:

> 'It was pretty good. It's just one of those things – you get out of the country and it's all you can think about.'

Which means that while, for example, that other well-known British hostage Terry Waite had his faith in God to sustain him in his long captivity, this particular very British hero whiled away some of the endless hours of solitude by dreaming of Marmite. And the key point being not that one particular individual in conditions of extreme jeopardy should turn to the thought of Marmite for solace, but that almost every Briton who read that gloriously stoic and deadpan quote knew exactly where the man, who had clearly endured so much, was coming from.

In recent times the popularity of Marmite has also been encouraged and enhanced by a series of brilliant advertising campaigns. Currently still running are the twin concepts that you either 'Love It' or 'Hate It'. That a company should promote its product by highlighting the fact that a large proportion of its potential consumers can't abide the stuff is, in marketing terms, a stroke of genius.

Equally witty, though far less well-known, is the creation of MarmArt – an online parody of New York's MoMart (Museum of Modern Art) that solely features works of art created using Marmite applied to slices of toast. To fully deconstruct the levels of meaning inherent in such an essentially British phenomenon would take a very long time indeed.

Without doubt, the Damien Hirst-like leading lights of the whole MarmArt Movement are the conceptual artists Fran & Kate, whose *London Skyline* is a quintich of five slices of toast that brilliantly depicts, amongst other landmarks, Tower Bridge, the Gherkin, the London Eye and the Millennium Dome. The fact that the Saatchi Gallery attempted to purchase the artwork for their permanent collection only seeks to highlight just how cutting edge, and collectable, this whole paradigm has become. The story that the artists responded to this unwanted approach by the forces of commercialisation by eating their art are unsubstantiated. If true, however, many experts believe that this may well mark for the artists an exciting departure from the conceptual field and into the arena of performance art.

~ 80 ~

If fox hunting is banned why do people still hunt foxes?

This is a prime example of the preservation of a great British tradition. It is a tradition with hundreds of years of history behind it that was in danger of falling foul of the so-called 'modern' views of an urban elite that had no inkling of the importance of continuity in maintaining the essential character of our great nation.

The British tradition in question is not the tradition of wearing red coats called pinks and chasing a fox around on horseback, but the far more important one commonly known as The Great British Compromise. Great British Compromises have been a part of this country for centuries. Without the Great British Compromise the country itself would be a very different place. For example, when faced with the seemingly irreconcilable choice of having the country run by an elected parliament or a hereditary monarch, the British, being the British, opted for a compromise and said let's have both. Or, more recently, take our attitude to Europe. Both major political parties hold to a line that essentially has it that we are both a part of Europe, and apart from Europe.

So for a long time compromise has been a big feature in our national make up. But in recent years the government had become worried that we weren't making as many compromises as before. Even the appointment of a Compromises Tsar had little effect in turning around the decline. As a last resort what the government realised was needed was an eye-catching compromise initiative that would highlight once and for all the true importance of the tradition of the Great British Compromise. As a result they have managed to create circumstances in which fox hunting is both against the law, and legal. And so a great British tradition was saved for the benefit and enjoyment of generations to come.

NB: Rumours that the other reason that the fox-hunting ban hasn't been the most banny of bans was because the government caved in after Bryan Ferry's son Terry had threatened to invade Parliament Square and set up a continuous free festival for lots of people called Quentin and Jasper, with himself leading a 'tribute' band called Foxy Music, are totally unfounded.

~ 81 ~

Where do the following British regional breads or cakes come from?

1 Stottie cake
2 Laver bread
3 Sally Lunn
4 Farl
5 Huffkin

ANSWERS.

1. The Stottie cake comes from the north-east of England.
2. Laver bread is made in Wales.
3. A Sally Lunn is a type of bun made in Bath.
4. Farl comes from Northern Ireland.
5. The Huffkin comes from Oscar's Bakery, 3 Limes Place, Preston Street, Faversham, Kent. Ask for Martin.

~ 82 ~

Who is the most important comedian in Britain today?

The funniest comedian is Peter Kay. The angriest is Mark Steel. The most influential is Vic Reeves. The grumpiest is Jack Dee. The cleverest is Stephen Fry. The most talented is Victoria Wood. The most deadpan is Jimmy Carr. The gag master is Ken Dodd. The most physical is Lee Evans. The most profound is Paul Whitehouse. The most underrated is Ronnie Ancona. The most powerful is Ricky Gervais. The most dangerous is Johnny Vegas. The most surreal are The Mighty Boosh. The wittiest is Paul Merton. And the creator of the zeitgeist-defining character is Catherine Tate.

The most important, however, are the ones who have reinvigorated comedy's power to tackle the most controversial subjects of the age, no matter the taboos that are transgressed in the process. The comedians in question are the imaginary young British Muslim duo who style themselves as 'The Two Iranis' and have set themselves the audacious task of cocking a snook at the excesses of radical Islam. Irani Burker and Irani Coran first came to prominence when their slapstick show examining the process of radicalisation called *Mum's Gone To Islam* was controversially left off the shortlist for the Perrier Award for Comedy at 2005 Edinburgh Fringe Festival.

The ensuing furore did wonders for their profile and, after a bidding war, they were snapped up by the BBC, for whom they were commissioned to write, star in and direct a series of 45-minute shows entitled *Friendly Fire*. However the shows were pulled by the powers that be in the BBC after a viewing of the pilot episode which ended with a musical skit that had the two Iranis performing as a lovesick pair of suicide bombers called Sunni and Shia serenading one another with the song 'I Got You Babe' in front of a back projection of actual bombings and their horrendous aftermath. For some reason this was thought to be in bad taste. But the best satire often is.

Luckily the money that was saved enabled the Corporation to commission a new series of *The Vicar Of Dibley* in which they reconfirmed their commitment to ethnic minority comedy by introducing the character of a black cleaner for the village hall.

Who was Sir Oswald Muesli?

Sir Oswald Muesli was a British politician who, in the 1930s, attempted to convert the British populous to that most un-British and fascistic of breakfasts – muesli. That muesli is fascistic is undeniable. For a start it's brown. And ugly. And hails from a part of Europe not really famed for its embrace of the joys of multiculturalism. Indeed the very act of eating the stuff involves a chomp, chomp, chomping action of the jaw that rhythmically echoes the goose-stepping marching beat of the jackboot.

Then there's the whole dubious philosophical side to the stuff. Muesli will keep you pure. In body and mind. It is cleansing. It purges your body of undesirable elements. And it sets you apart from others who indulge in breakfasts that they endeavour to actually enjoy. Yes, muesli is the breakfast of the True Believer.

While outwardly a somewhat respectable figure, Sir Oswald was, in fact, as mad as a bagful of one-eyed cats trapped inside a spin dryer. He wanted nothing more than to turn Britain into a brown-shirted and brown-trousered (for obvious reasons) nation of intolerant, super-fit, puritanical fascists. And muesli was his weapon of choice. It was, in so many ways, an attack from the rear.

But fool that he was, he underestimated the common sense, and the common decency, of the British working man. So when Sir Oswald and his cohorts marched through the East End of London handing out samples and exhorting the masses to embrace the joys of muesli he was confronted, appropriately enough in Cable Street, by a phalanx of Eastenders who gave the hateful oaf and his followers the thrashing they so richly deserved and then chucked the muesli in the Thames. Indeed even to this day, when the tide is out, remnants of that self-same muesli can still be found scattered about the foreshore of the river.

After inflicting the decisive defeat on Sir Oswald, the victorious Londoners repaired to the local caffs for the traditional Breakfast Of The Free. That's why egg, bacon, a fried slice and a tea with two sugars isn't just food.

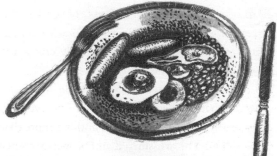

A full English

It's a political celebration by the British of our rights as individuals to be individuals and to lead lives free from oppression, hate, and the control of those who are supposedly better than us who want to tell us how to live, what to think, and worst of all, what to have for breakfast.

~ 84 ~

What is the seventh verse
of the national anthem?

'Oh! Now some people say,
Young Charles is run away,
Over to France;
'Cause he was sore afraid,
Of valiant Marshall Wade,
For if that he had staid,
He'd stood no chance.'

~ 85 ~

Is the hokey-cokey really what it's all about?

The hokey-cokey is an honest to goodness, old-time, singalong song beloved, supposedly, of yer 'onest to goodness, old-time, pie, mash and liquor-munching cockneys. The lyrics, while hardly rivalling Sondheim in their intricacies, do exert a certain naïve charm. What elevates the song to a whole new level of meaning are the accompanying dance moves.

For any newcomer to Britain knowledge of the words, music and actions would undoubtedly be a boon in their attempts at integration.

The lyrics are as follows:

You put your left arm in
You put your left arm out
In, out, in, out
You shake it all about
You do the hokey-cokey
And you turn around
That's what it's all about
Ohhhhhhhhhhh! The hokey-cokey!

Ohhhhhhhhhh! The hokey-cokey!
Ohhhhhhhhhh! The hokey-cokey!
Knees bend
Arms stretch
Rah! Rah! Rah!

The actions for the most part mirror the instructions laid out in the lyrics. But before the song starts the group of people doing the hokey-cokey must arrange themselves in a circle. Incidentally, the hokey-cokey has to be done by a group of people. Attempt a solo rendition of the dance and you will look very foolish indeed. (This is in marked contrast to the group endeavour where, admittedly, you will still look foolish, but so does everyone else.)

Once the circle has been established, the song can begin.

When the line '*You put your left arm in*' is sung you, somewhat unsurprisingly, put your left arm in. Then, following the prescriptive through-line of the lyric, you put it out, then put it in-out, in-out, before finally shaking it all about.

Next, on the line '*You do the hokey-cokey*', you clasp your hands together in front of you, at chest height, with interlocking fingers, and proceed to rock them from left to right.

Then, on the instruction, '*You turn around*', you do just that.

Before the next line is sung everyone in the circle joins hands and, in time to the rising crescendo of *'Ohhhhhhhhh!'*, the entire group moves towards the centre of the circle, hence making the circle considerably smaller. However, the circle expands back to its original size while the refrain of *'The hokey-cokey!'* is delivered.

This sequence of actions is repeated twice more during the subsequent lines.

Once the circle has returned to its starting positions the somewhat subdued coda of *'Knees bend, arms stretch, Rah! Rah! Rah!'* with appropriately accompanying actions completes the first cycle of the song.

The song then continues in this fashion with the listing of other bodily parts. Commonly these include the right arm, the left leg and the right leg.

The song reaches an often frenzied climax as participants are entreatied to put their *'whole self in…'* which once again concludes with the affirmation that *'that's what it's all about'*.

The song was very popular in wartime Britain. Mind you, back then, television hadn't really got going and no one had heard of Sudoku.

The origins of the hokey-cokey are a matter of considerable debate. Various people have claimed authorship, including the Irish songwriter Jimmy Kennedy who also penned both 'We're gonna hang out the washing on the Siegfried Line' and 'The Teddy Bears' Picnic'. However references to a similar song and, indeed, dance, crop up far earlier. Some scholars cite as a possible source a Shaker song entitled 'Hinkum-Booby' that was written down in the eighteenth century, while the dance, or a variation of it, has been traced back a century before that.

However Jimmy Kennedy's claim was strengthened on the day of his funeral when the undertakers came to put his body into the coffin. The trouble started when first they put his left leg in. As a result the funeral cortege was somewhat late arriving at the church.

Interestingly, the Oxford English Dictionary states that the term *hokey-cokey* is derived from the music hall magician's incantation of *hocus-pocus*. This, in turn, is thought to be a corruption of the Latin phrase *hoc enim est corpus meum* – which translates as 'this is my body'. It is a phrase used by Roman Catholic priests at the central point in a mass. This is the moment in the proceedings at which the host – representing the bread broken at the Last Supper – is supposed to be transubstantiated into the Body Of Christ.

This central tenet of faith for Catholics was mocked by the Puritans as being nonsensical bogus magic. By appropriating and subverting the words involved into the phrase 'hocus-pocus' the Puritans thus hoped to ridicule the beliefs of their rivals.

Canon Nairn Briggs has even taken this analysis a stage further by suggesting that the actions of the song 'The Hokey-Cokey' were derived from a physical parody of the actions of the priest during the rituals of the Latin mass.

If this is true, then the primary-coloured Tweenies Bella, Fizz, Jake and Milo are, each time they sing the song on children's TV, nothing more than a bunch of dogma disseminating anti-papist propagandists out to brainwash the vulnerable and impressionable minds of this nation's toddlers to such an extent that it is only a matter of time before the youngsters march on every Catholic church in the land making a pyre of their rusks and dummies and burning the incumbent priests at the stake whilst gleefully shouting 'Rah! Rah! Rah!'

Then again, this may well be overstating the dangers of allowing cherub-faced little kiddies to sing 'The Hokey-Cokey' whilst watching the telly.

But deconstruct the nature of the hokey-cokey still further and, satirical origins aside, it reveals itself as nothing more than a formalised, almost tribal, assertion of membership.

To start with the participants form an inward-looking circle. This, obviously, symbolises belonging. Equally obviously if all the people in the circle belong, then all those outside it do not. Then the actions, though ostensibly meaningless, are a ritual. And if you both know, and participate in, the steps of the ritual you are, once again, asserting that you are part of the group.

Finally, ponder on the deeper meaning of the words and what other interpretation can there be of the climactic stanza's assertion that putting 'your whole self in' is 'what it's all about' than as nothing less than a heroic demand that one commit one's self wholeheartedly to whatever endeavour one is engaged upon.

Analysed in these terms it becomes clear that the hokey-cokey is, in essence, a glorious celebration of the bonds of belonging and a subtly coded secular hymn to the philosophical and practical benefits of commitment.

All of which means that, depending on your own views of the meaning of life, the hokey-cokey may well be what it's all about.

~ 86 ~

*In 1967 how many holes were
there in Blackburn, Lancashire? Did
this number include golf courses?*

On the 17th of January 1967 there were, according to
the *Daily Mail*, four thousand holes in Blackburn,
Lancashire. This number did not include golf courses
even though the town at the time boasted three separate
courses dating back to the 1890s within its municipal
boundaries. The figure of four thousand worked out, for
the residents of Blackburn, at a per capita rate of one
twenty-sixth of a hole per person.

As to the related question that was posed not long
after as to how many holes it would take to fill the Albert
Hall, the simple answer is, of course, one. It would just
have to be big enough.

Which is the correct spelling, *Boadicea* or *Boudica*?

Boadicea or Boudica was a queen of the ancient British Iceni tribe that ruled Norfolk. In AD60 she led her people in an uprising against the occupying Romans. Initially she was successful. But inevitably the revolt ended in failure. As a result she was put to death. As time passed she was, to a large extent, forgotten in the annals of British history. Her resurrection came primarily in the Victorian era. In that time, for obvious reasons, the idea of a indomitable British queen became popular in the extreme.

As to the correct way to spell her name, the answer favoured by most historians these days is Boudica. Boadicea is now thought to be a Middle Ages mistranslation of a manuscript of Tacitus. However, all through the Victorian Age, to hundreds of thousands of British schoolchildren she was Boadicea. And as the legend of Boadicea is largely one that seized the Victorian imagination there is a reasonable argument to be made to suggest that she should remain Boadicea.

Indeed recent research in the Norfolk village of Mundesley has uncovered inside a mountain cave a faded muriel that appears to depict a fearsome horde of Iceni menfolk heading into battle chanting:

> 'Woad Army! Woad Army!
> Boadicea's Woad and White Army!'

Obviously this blood-curdling chant would have been rendered somewhat less effective if the correct pronounciation of the name had been Boudica. After all were the Romans really going to be frightened by an enemy who couldn't even get their war chants to scan properly?

~ 88 ~

Who is the 'one' who has been barred from All Bar One?

This is a tricky one to answer. In reality no 'one' has been barred. No doubt, however, that at individual branches of this all-conquering chain of hostelries, individuals have been barred. But there is not in place a universal ban on one, specific, individual.

Having said this, outside busy All Bar Ones on Friday and Saturday nights, bouncers are employed. And they do bar people from entry. Over the course of a single evening they will invariably bar more than one individual. So, in truth, the door policy of these places is 'all bar several'. Presumably this wasn't chosen as the name of the chain as it sounds somewhat odd. But then again, is there much sense in naming a chain of bars after a door policy? You might as well call the place 'No Jeans Or Trainers'.

Despite all this, All Bar Ones are undoubtedly a success. And it may well that their name, subliminally, has contributed to that success. This is because the name manages to resolve two seemingly irreconcilable desires of the British drinker. Their egalitarian nature wishes for a place where everyone is welcome. But they also nurture a desire for a degree of exclusivity.

All Bar One satisfies both desires.

And just so long as you don't roll up in the wrong kind of clothes, or already drunk, you won't be the one who is barred. But should you wish to drink in a place that posseses individual character, you could do worse than bar yourself.

~ 89 ~

How much personal space should I leave between myself and my fellow Britons?

Seven and three quarter inches. (That's measuring nose to nose).

~ 90 ~

For what are the following British small towns and villages best known?

1 Royston Vasey
2 Hustings
3 Robson Green
4 Chesney Hawkes
5 Kingston Trio

It has often been said that while Britain's thriving metropolises are the powerhouses of the nation's social, economic and cultural ennui it is, by contrast, in the small towns and villages that hidden yet key facets of this great land's subconscious personality can be found. As such, an understanding of the delights some of these places offer is invaluable in helping a newcomer to fully understand just how big a mouthful they have bitten off in their quest to integrate.

1 *Royston Vasey* is a delightful North-country village famed for its friendliness. Even the village sign boasts the legend 'Welcome To Royston Vasey. You'll never leave.' If you do visit the village make

sure you pop into the local shop run by Edward and his sister Tubbs and mention that you're a tourist. They love making a fuss of newcomers.

2   *Hustings* is a small, genteel seaside resort town located on the south coast of England. It is the town that local constituency MPs retreat to between elections. (NB: This also explains why they are never seen between elections.) In Hustings the elusive MPs spend their time working on their expenses claims, practicing jeering for their annual attendance at a House of Commons debate, and perfecting the art of only knocking on doors of people who agree with them.

3   *Robson Green* is an exclusive enclave of the ever-expanding town of Mediachester. Its inhabitants are characterised by their ubiquitousness. For reasons that are often hard to discern these people tend to pop up everywhere. Current inhabitants include Russell Brand, Sharon Osbourne, Gordon Ramsay, Mylene Klass, Kwame Kwei-Armah and the rostrum cameraman Ken Morse. It is interesting to note, however, that residency in Robson Green often doesn't last very long.

4   *Chesney Hawkes* is a town trapped in a bubble of irony. For example, the local steak house is run by

Mrs L. McCartney. The pub is called the Temperance Arms. And local bye-laws insist that Mr Azgodintended, the plastic surgeon, can only perform breast enhancement operations on Shrove Tuesday. Incidentally, Chesney Hawkes is where Alanis Morissette got married. It rained.

5 *Kingston Trio* is a small village that was created on the edge of the up-market town of Kingston upon Thames in the 1950s. It was designed and built to house the predominantly Jamaican West Indians who were enticed to the area to work on the buses and in the labour-starved National Health Service in the post-war decade. Ostensibly the village's separateness was promoted as a way of 'helping the incomers feel at home'. However, it soon became apparent that the real motive was far less benevolent. Over the years, of course, attitudes have changed. Integration has occurred, helped in the early days by the Kingston Trionian's habit of bursting into impromptu cheery calypso songs. Favourite ditties included 'When De Wind Rushes In', 'Dogs And Irish Welcome', and 'The River Of Blood Calypso'.

~ 91 ~

What is the most useful bit of advice available in Britain today?

Have you tried turning it off and turning it on again?

~ 92 ~

In Britain how many inquiries into a war does it take to get to the bottom of why that war went so badly wrong?

More than four.

That's because there have been four inquiries into the war in Iraq already and still, for the most part, the British public haven't got anywhere near a complete or satisfying picture of what went on. There has been the Foreign Affairs Committee Inquiry into the decision to go to war in Iraq, there has been the Intelligence and Security Committee Inquiry into Iraqi weapons of mass destruction, there has been the Hutton Inquiry into the circumstances surrounding the death of David Kelly and there has been the Butler Review of intelligence on weapons of mass destruction.

This clearly is an appalling state of affairs. The responsible people should be held to account and, if found wanting, be made to resign. Four inquiries and still no satisfactory answers? Since when did Britain become so bad at inquiries? The only sensible response is for there to be a public inquiry into why all the inquiries went so pear-shaped.

Then the fundamental failings in the thinking that lead up to the decision to launch the inquiries will become clear. Not that the people in the front line of the inquiries were solely, or even primarily, to blame as they were just doing their jobs. The fault undoubtedly lies further up the inquiry command chain. The erroneous premise on the basis of which the inquiries were launched in the first place must bear a large burden of responsibility. And the scandalous neglect of planning for what to do after the inquiries had been completed must be shown up for the very predictable disaster in waiting that it so obviously was.

A sign

If Britain is to hold its head high in the international community once again it must never again launch such an ill-conceived and poorly thought-through series of inquiries.

*Can you match the following
members of the Tracy family to
their respective Thunderbirds?*

ⓐ Gordon
ⓑ Scott
ⓒ Alan
ⓓ John
ⓔ Virgil

Gordon was in charge of Thunderbird Four, Scott flew Thunderbird One, Alan was the astronaut of the spaceship Thunderbird Three, John manned the space-station Thunderbird Five, and Virgil ferried the equipment to whatever disaster site they were targeting in Thunderbird Two.

As most of the time it was Thunderbirds One and Two that handled the bulk of the rescues, small boys with short trousers and scabby knees would contest the right to be Scott or Virgil in countless playgrounds the length and breadth of the country. No one ever wanted to be John Tracy, who was forever doomed to a solitary existence circling the planet in Thunderbird Five waiting to pick up international distress calls. Indeed, as the small boys with short trousers and scabby knees got a bit older they would often wonder just what familial crime John had committed to warrant his perpetual banishment from the tropical island paradise that was Tracy Island.

Psychologically this made John Tracy by far the most interesting and complex of the family. There he was, up in space, all alone, circling the planet, listening out for those in need of rescue, yet who was there to listen to his own deeply buried but very real need for help, for companionship, for human warmth? Who would be listening if John Tracy made a distress call? And who would come to his rescue?

Unfortunately such profound, psychological matters were not really in the remit of the show which tended to focus on rescuing people trapped in burning skyscrapers, small boys pinned down by support beams in abandoned mineshafts and, in the seminal *Attack of the Alligators*, misguided scientists trapped in swampland houses by giant alligators.

The two other key characters of Thunderbirds were the precisely accented English aristocrat Lady Penelope, and Parker, the chauffeur of her iconic pink Rolls-Royce.

How influential this erstwhile children's TV show was in British life can be judged by the fact that Noel Gallagher, the driving force behind the leading Britpop beat combo Oasis, clearly modelled much of his look on Parker. On top of this, when the children who had grown up watching the cool authority of Lady Penelope attained voting age in a country that was seemingly in a terminal state of decline they elected a certain Mrs Thatcher to be Prime Minister.

Admittedly Mrs Thatcher never actually drove round the country in a pink Rolls-Royce, but for much of her time in office, her Cabinet, and indeed vast parts of the nation as a whole, did affect a demeanour that amounted to little more than a muttered:

'Yes, m'lady.'

~ 94 ~

Who is the more successful of the Attenborough Boys, David or Dickie?

Richard Samuel Attenborough was born on 29 August 1923 in Cambridge. He has won two Oscars, three Golden Globes and four BAFTAs. He has also been the chairman of Channel Four, the chairman of Capital Radio, the chairman of Goldcrest Films, the president of RADA, the president of BAFTA, the president of the British National Film and Television School, and the president of the Gandhi Foundation. However, it hasn't all been good, as he's also been a director of Chelsea Football Club. In 1967 he was awarded the CBE, he was knighted in 1976, and in 1993 he was made a life peer as Baron Attenborough of Richmond.

He first came to prominence as an actor in 1942 playing a deserting sailor in the film *In Which We Serve*. His real breakthrough happened five years later, playing the psychopathic gangster Pinky in the 1947 film of Graham Greene's *Brighton Rock*. He worked continually in the then still-thriving British film industry and in the late 1950s set up Beaver Films with the director Bryan Forbes that produced, amongst other things, the classic *Whistle Down The Wind*.

In 1969 Richard Attenborough turned his considerable talents towards directing for the first time and successfully managed to transfer the hit musical *Oh! What a Lovely War* to the big screen. He subsequently directed *Young Winston* and *A Bridge Too Far*. But it was his 1982 historical epic *Gandhi* that cemented his reputation as a cinematic giant. The film won eight Oscars including Best Film and Best Direction.

Despite the fact that he is in his eighties, he is still making films such as *Closing The Ring*, a movie set in Belfast during the Second World War.

If one man can ever be held to represent a whole industry, it is Lord Attenborough and the British film industry. And if there were any more honours the country could bestow upon him, it surely would. But short of discovering some quirk of lineage that actually proves he, and not Prince Charles, should be next in line for the throne, there is very little left the nation can give him.

Richard Attenborough's brother David was born on 8 May in London in 1926. He too has been knighted and lists after his name the honours OM, CH, CVO, CBE and FRS. On top of all this, a 2006 survey in *Reader's Digest* accorded him the heady accolade of being the most trusted celebrity in Britain. But this does him too little credit as he is probably, in truth, the most trusted person in Britain.

David's interest in nature burgeoned at an early age and by the time he was seven years old he had already amassed a fine collection of natural specimens. Having won a scholarship to Clare College at Cambridge University he nurtured his passion by studying Natural Sciences. After two years' National Service in the Royal Navy he tried his hand in publishing before joining the BBC's factual broadcasting department of the nascent television service. Soon he became a producer and over-saw both quiz and music shows.

However it was a three-part series *The Pattern of Animals,* which he both produced and presented, that first brought his love of animals to the small screen. As it turned out it was to be a match made in heaven. (Or whatever the TV equivalent of heaven is.) Next, in 1954, came *Zoo Quest,* a show he presented only because the person who was scheduled to do so fell ill.

Not content with making programmes David Attenborough made his creative mark across a whole channel when he became Controller of BBC2 between 1965 and 1969. During that time he commissioned the likes of *The Ascent Of Man, Civilisation, Masterclass, Man Alive* and *The Money Programme.* But his vision was far wider than these highbrow programmes indicate. Under his watch *The Old Grey Whistle Test* was launched, as were *The Likely Lads, Not Only...But Also,* and, in a move that was to eventually change a nation's Saturday night for ever, *Match Of The Day.* He even saw the televisual possi-bility in the then-minor sport of snooker once the chan-nel started to broadcast in colour.

Despite all these achievements, it is for his 1979 series *Life On Earth* that he is best remembered. There are very few masterpieces in the world of television, but this was one. It did nothing less than show the splendours of the natural world in all their amazing glory. It took the nature documentary format and turned it into a compelling, life-enhancing journey of discovery. At a time when conservation was starting to be recognised for the necessity it is, Attenborough's series highlighted just what we were running the risk of losing if we did not think again about how we lived on the planet. Subsequent series have been just as good, but it was the first one that set the incredibly high standard.

For many viewers the highlight of the first series was Attenborough's encounter with lowland gorillas. To mingle with these seemingly almost human creatures he had to learn their ways, understand their mating rituals, and become au fait with their complex hierarchies and belligerent displays of power. It's interesting to note that it was around this time that David's brother Richard was having to press the flesh in Hollywood in order to raise the finance for *Gandhi*. Whether the two compared notes has never been recorded.

Strangely, David Attenborough's latest series crosses over into what is his brother's territory. *Life In Cold Blood* is a documentary series that explores the intricate web of life that exists in the little examined, and little understood, world of people making films about Truman Capote's best-known work.

Given such a roll-call of groundbreaking work it is easy to see why many people judge Sir David Attenborough to be the most important broadcaster that this country has ever produced, or will ever produce. But perhaps the greatest accolade ever accorded to the man is to have one of only four remaining species of echidna named after him. The *Zaglossus attenboroughi* lives in New Guinea and glories under the common (though obviously not that common) name of Sir David's Long-Beaked echidna.

Compare the triumphs of the two Attenborough brothers and it is hard to know which has achieved the most. Probably the only way to settle the matter is if the

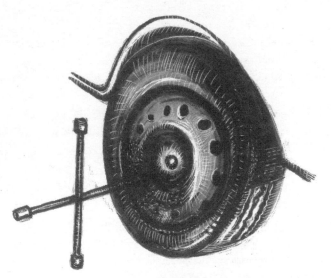

A wheel

two of them had a fight. But, for many reasons, this is unlikely to happen. Also, in order to answer our original question, such a battle is unnecessary. That's because in Britain there is a strong streak of modesty running through the national character which recognises that lives lived away from the glare of the public eye are just as important as those who garner plaudits and awards at every turn. Which is why many a true Briton will smile a smile of quiet satisfaction when we state that, in fact, the more successful of the Attenborough Boys is neither Richard or David, but the third brother, John, who made his career in the motor trade.

~ 95 ~

How do you distinguish Ant from Dec?

It doesn't really matter.

~ 96 ~

Why are the British obsessed with talking about the weather?

In Britain, talking about the weather has very little to do with the weather. Instead it is a way of easing out of the embarrassed silence that often occurs whenever two Britons meet. As such it is a codified exchange, the significance of which is not the actual words that are spoken, but the fact that something has been spoken.

In many ways it is the conversational equivalent of offering someone a cup of tea. It is a ritual that acts as an initial point of contact between the two participants. Once the formalities of the ritual have been observed the conversation can then cut to more important matters. For example, the following dialogue clearly illustrates just how useful such an exchange can be.

Person A: Hasn't it been cold recently?

Person B: Yes it has. Dreadful.

Person A: I know, I know but what can you do?

Person B: Get the jumpers out, I suppose.

Person A: Yeah…hmm… I was sorry to hear that your father had died.

Person B: Thank you.

Obviously, this is a fairly extreme example. But it does indicate how a banal exchange about the weather can act as a gently shelving beach against which can lap a whole ocean of, in this case, grief.

Thankfully, most conversations about the weather tend to end up somewhere far more mundane. And some, indeed, go no further than the weather. But in Britain, this too is perfectly acceptable. This is because despite us all being crammed together on a relatively small island, we've never really figured out how to get on with one another. So anything that eases our embarrassment in a whole plethora of social situations is gratefully clung to.

If, as a newcomer to Britain, you do ever find yourself at a loss as to what to say in any particular situation, just turn the conversation to the weather. It'll work every time. For example:

Person A: Hasn't it been cold recently?
Person B: Yes it has. Dreadful.
Person A: I know, I know but what can you do?
Person B: Get the jumpers out, I suppose.
Person A: Yeah…hmm…So, did you come?
Person B: No, not really.
Person A: Oh, well never mind.
Person B: Yeah, never mind.

~ 97 ~

Who is the quintessential British hero?

Scott of the Antarctic is the quintessential British hero. This is for the three following reasons.

1 He failed.
2 He died.
3 He was attempting an endeavour that was, essentially, pointless.

~ 98 ~

What is the 'Must Have Queue'?

The Must Have Queue is the highest form of that great British institution – the queue. Ostensibly it purports to be a linear arrangement of people lining up to get their hands on whatever is, at that particular moment, the Must Have item of the day. In recent times these items have included Sainsbury's Anya Hindmarsh bag, the latest Harry Potter, or anything from Kate Moss's designer collection at Topshop.

Less perceptive observers of the British social scene have taken this to be an indictment of the increasing shallowness of British society. But this flawed analysis misses the point of what is really going on. In reality, it is not the achievement of acquiring the object in question that provides the most reward for the Must Have Queuer, rather it is the experience of being in the queue itself.

The Must Have Queue combines camaraderie, with competitiveness, and the satisfaction of having committed yourself to a cause that requires a level of determination that takes you out of the comfort zone of everyday life. For some there's also the possibility of later zeitgeistian financial reward when they flog whatever they've managed to buy on eBay. (But the significance of this is greatly exaggerated.) There is also the subtle thrill that comes with exclusivity. After all, in most cases, in a very short space of time, more of the 'exclusive' items will be made available, but only a relatively select band of people will have been stupid enough to queue up all night to get them before everyone else.

But beyond all these attributes of the Must Have Queue is the subsequent contemplation by the Must Have Queuer of the absurdity of it all. Years after the bag has been chucked in a (plastic) bin-bag, the dress has disintegrated in the wash, and Harry Potter has been dispatched to Oxfam by indifference – an enemy far more deadly than Voldemort – the Must Have Queuer will disbelievingly contemplate how ridiculous they must have been to have succumbed to the hype and joined that queue. And that's when the Must Have Queue will have finally served its true, profound, purpose. It will have enabled the Queuer to take stock of what had been, and what is, really important in their life.

So while whatever it is you buy when you eventually get to the front of the Must Have Queue is rarely worth the wait, the act of waiting itself will have definitely been worth it.

And, as the more philosophically minded amongst you will have no doubt noticed, as a subtle metaphor for life itself, the Must Have Queue is hard to beat.

~ 99 ~

Why is the conga such a popular dance in Britain?

This is because the conga is the only dance that combines dancing with queueing.

~ 100 ~

What is the difference between Pinter and panto?

Harold Pinter is the presiding genius of British theatre. He has produced a vastly influential body of work the precise meaning of which has always been hard to pin down. Plays like *The Birthday Party*, *The Caretaker*, and *The Homecoming*, in which apparently innocent situations become threatening, soon came to be described as 'comedies of menace' (as opposed to the more conventional 'comedies of manners'). In truth the struggle to pin down precisely what any particular Pinter play is about is fruitless, and may well be pointless.

Pinter himself has, however, described his earlier plays as metaphors about power and powerlessness. Although he rarely explains his work, he did describe a scene in *The Birthday Party* in which the characters Goldberg and McCann menacingly, and for no apparent reason, interrogate the character Stanley, as being an exploration of the way in which certain forces within society want to snuff out dissent and silence the voices of individuals.

Pinter is also known for his precise use of language. But he is more famous for his supposedly excessive use, in dialogue, of pauses. Indeed parodists often think that just by employing a lot of … pauses … in a piece of … dialogue they have produced something … Pinter-esque. Obviously this is a banal pantomime of what Pinter does.

To understand what is really going on you need to turn to a speech that Pinter gave at the National Student Drama Festival in 1962. Here he talks about two kinds of silences : 'one where no word is spoken' the other 'when perhaps a torrent of language is being employed'. In the first the silence speaks volumes, in the second the volumes are really silence. So, by solely focusing on Pinter's pauses where no words are said is to miss Pinter's equally important pauses when words are pouring forth from the actor's mouths. Or, as he summed it up in that 1962 address, 'one way of looking at speech is to say that it is a constant stratagem to cover nakedness'.

Once, when questioned about the meaning of his work, Pinter off-handedly remarked that it was all about the cocktail cabinet hidden under the weasel. Although this was meant as a throwaway comment, and is one that he subsequently disowned, many critics took this as an enlightened summary of his work. But even the most cursory consideration of the comment reveals it as being absurd. After all, for a cocktail cabinet to fit under a weasel it would have to be a very small cocktail cabinet. Or a very large weasel. And if that were the case we would probably be straying into Ionesco territory.

Even the very word Pinteresque is remarkable. To

have an adjective based on your name is undoubtedly an accolade. One few writers are afforded. There's Shakespearean, Dickensian, Chekovian, Audenary and not many others. However before the adjective Pinteresque was arrived at, several options were mooted. Many cultural critics argued the case for Pinterssential, some favoured Pintacular, and the mass-market tabloids championed the cause of the artisan simplicity of Pintery. In the end Pinteresque won out, although there was a spirited late challenge, mainly from the great and the good of the acting fraternity, to have the slow-fire dialogue of the early plays referred to as Pinter-Patter.

In more recent years Pinter's plays, and his work in general, have become overtly political. If the earlier plays were metaphors about power and powerlessness, his later works sought to present the realities of power and its abuses. His growing and impassioned disquiet with the world as he sees it is perhaps best summed up in the lecture he gave after winning the Nobel Prize for Literature. Entitled *Art, Truth & Politics* it highlighted the disparity between the search for truth in art, and the avoidance of truth in politics.

'Political language, as used by politicians, does not venture into any of this territory (of the artist) since the majority of politicians, on the evidence available to us, are interested not in truth but in power and in the mainte-nance of that power. To maintain that power it is essen-tial that people remain in ignorance, that they live in ignorance of the truth, even the truth of their own lives. What surrounds us therefore is a vast tapestry of lies, upon which we feed.'

And in an explicit criticism of America and its foreign policy objectives and practices he returned, forty-three years on, to the idea that speech is 'a constant stratagem to cover nakedness' when he stated that in the USA 'language is actually used to keep thought at bay'.

Unfortunately as Pinter's plays have become more political, they have become less popular. But what he is saying now is far more important than what he was saying then.

Panto, on the face of it, is something completely different to Pinter. Panto is short for pantomime, which is a traditional British theatrical entertainment of broad comedy, farce, music, stock roles and topical jokes. It is performed at Christmas and is predominantly aimed at children. Its current form dates back to Victorian days, with strong music-hall influences. But its roots run far deeper.

In the run-up to Christmas two hundred pantos run concurrently throughout the country and it has been estimated that they account for up to twenty per cent of all the theatrical performances in the UK in any one year. What is undoubtedly true is that for many people in Britain a pantomime was their first ever experience of live theatre.

It is commonly accepted that the origins of

pantomime in this country date back to the early 1700s when commedia dell'arte players, from French fairgrounds, arrived in London to put on what were termed 'night scenes'. It has been argued that their easy to understand style developed because the troupes were Italian performers who had been trying to entertain unsophisticated French fairgoers. With no common language, simple plots and liberal use of non-verbal gagging became imperative. As a result what was created was a form of theatre that could travel internationally.

On arrival in London the potential appeal of this style of performance lead a dancing master called John Weaver to work it into a 'ballet' that he staged at Drury Lane in 1716. But the form really took off as a mass-market popular entertainment in 1723 with the staging of *The Necromancer or Harlequin's Dr Faustus*. As with any success in the world of popular theatre, imitators soon abounded.

The shows that the paying public flocked to see usually took the following form. The opening scene would be one taken from classical mythology. This would be followed by a transformation of characters into such types as Columbine, Pantaloon and Harlequin, and the second half would develop into a knockabout harlequinade.

By the start of the 1800s the mythological opening had been replaced by a fairytale one. Other traditions were also in place. The 'dame' character would be played by a man, the harlequin would wear a skintight suit of spangled lozenges, and the pantomimes were Christmas (and Easter) fare. In 1806 the comic Harlequin character evolved into a clown thanks to the genius of Joseph Grimaldi who brought the house down at Covent Garden in *Harlequin Mother Goose, or The Golden Egg*.

Pantomime always absorbed whatever were the latest crazes so in Victorian times elements of burlesque and operetta appeared. And certain stories became proven audience-pleasers. There was *Cinderella*, *Puss in Boots*, *The Babes in The Wood*, *Aladdin* and *Dick Whittington*. Characters such as Widow Twankey, Baron Hardup, Buttons and Whittington's Cat also became well-established. By then panto had become a purely Christmas tradition mainly aimed at juvenile audiences. However, perhaps in an attempt to evade the buttoned-up nature of the times, the hero became the 'principal boy' who was played by a woman in scandalously leg-hugging tights.

As different productions vied with each other to pull in the crowds producers tried to make their show more spectacular than their rivals. Sumptuous processions with elaborate costumes came in, as did intricate ballet and gasp-inducing aerial stunts. And 'celebrity casting' grew with famous performers imported from both burlesque and music hall. Audience participation also became an essential part of the whole experience*.

---

* Oh no it didn't!

In short, by the end of the Victorian era the style of pantomime as it is known today was pretty much in place. And while it may never have achieved high critical status it has always remained a supremely popular form of theatre. Indeed many repertory and regional theatres rely on the cash influx that pantomime generates to subsidise much of what they do during the rest of the year. Which means that while pantomime may not be high art, often it's the thing that pays for the high art.

So, while panto and Pinter are completely unconnected, a tenuous case can be made that without panto, there'd be no Pinter. Or not the Pinter as he is known today. Ridiculous though this argument clearly is it is also worth considering that Harold Pinter did start out as an actor. At the beginning of his career, having dropped out of RADA, it has been recorded that one of his earliest roles was in a Chesterfield Hippodrome production of *Dick Whittington and His Cat*.

There is, however, absolutely no truth in the rumour that the reason Pinter has recently stepped back from writing conventional plays is because he is working on a completely new form of theatrical entertainment based on pantomime. But it is a version of pantomime that draws heavily on both his earlier writing style and his current political concerns. What he is seeking to do is create a populist, mass appeal, entertainment that can carry explicit political messages. The result, while clearly owing many debts to panto is, in fact, the new theatrical hybrid of 'Pinto'. Although none of this is really happening, the following synopsis of the non-existent play and its imaginary production have leaked out.

The show is, allegedly, to be called *Dick Cheneyton and His Poodle*.

The hero of the story is Dick Cheneyton, an idealistic serial draft deferrer from the sticks who decides to go to Washington to make his fortune, as he has been told that the 'the streets of the Shining City On The Hill are paved with gold'. However, when he gets there he finds that all the deals for the gold paving have been tied up in a no-bid contract handed out by Alderman Rumsmell to a company that the Alderman himself owns. It is a rude awakening for the naïve young lad who turns his back on the corrupt city and sets off to walk home.

But half-way down Washington Hill he hears the sound of the Liberty Bell chiming and every clang of that great beacon of freedom seems to whisper in his ear 'Turn again Cheneyton, Twice alderman of Washington'.

Heeding the message Cheneyton returns to the city and sets about learning its ways and means. Though staying mainly behind the scenes he rises through the ranks of Alderman Rumsmell's household and ends up in charge. Along the way he acquires a faithful poodle called Tony. And before long Cheneyton, Rumsmell and Tony all come to work in the house of the dim-witted comedy character Idle W, who has inherited the city of Washington from his father.

One day, because they have nothing better to do, they all decide to go on a boat trip. Co-linda the Cook – hilariously played by a large, black, ex-general in a frock – advises them against it. But they never really pay him much heed. Before long a storm arises so strong that it knocks down buildings and blows them off course. In a blind panic they steer their boat where they can and end up beached on the coast of Barbary.

They make their way to the Sultan's Palace. Here they find the place overrun by rats, with court being held by their one-time friend Rattam the King Rat. Cheneyton, sensing an opportunity to do good in the world, sets his poodle on the rats. The rats soon run away. Even the once mighty King Rat is discovered cowering in a hole.

With the Palace cleared of vermin the Sultan – Demos – is reinstated by Dick Cheneyton, Idle W, Alderman Rumsmell, and Tony the Poodle. He is so grateful that everyone gets rewarded. Even Tony gets a new bone! Cheneyton and his friends return to Washington where they are feted as heroes.

Interestingly the first half of the show lasts forty-five minutes, while the second half seems to go on for ever. Pinter also employs many of the techniques for which he became famous. There are two types of silences. The first where nothing is being said, but a lot is going on. The second where a torrent of words mean nothing, like when in a brilliantly comical nonsense speech Alderman Rumsmell declares:

'As we know there are known knowns. These are the things we know we know. We also know there are known unknowns that is to say we know there are some things we don't know. But there are unknown unknowns, the ones we don't know we don't know...'

And he doesn't eschew the pantomime tradition of the simple line with a hidden, risqué, meaning that has the older, more sophisticated members of the audience laughing knowingly out loud. For example when, en route to the Sultan's Palace Co-linda, speaking from the wings, turns to the audience and says:

'Five miles from Baghdad and still no WMD!'

What is more unexpected is the way Pinter subtly changes the tone of some of his earlier work. For example, an interrogation scene set in the dungeons of Abu Gravy – Idle W: 'Why's it called Abu Gravy?' Alderman Rumsmell: (*Waving a four-page executive order*) 'Because everyone brown ends up covered in lumps!' – is, in part, a direct reference to the interrogation scene in *The Birthday Party*, but this time played for slapstick laughs.

Naturally there's also audience participation. But once again Pinter displays his genius by taking the convention and twisting it into something new. Having defeated the King Rat the triumphant quartet of

Cheneyton, Rumsmell, Idle W and Tony realise they
cannot maintain the powers they have accrued unless a
new threat stalks the world. So to encourage an oh-so-
useful climate of fear they enlist the audience in a bout of
traditional banter. Only this time the roles are reversed.

> Dick: Boys and Girls, Mums and Dads, Senators
>   and Representatives I'm really worried about
>   sneaky Terrorats. They're out to wreck our
>   homeland security. But with your help we can
>   hold them at bay. All *you've* got to do is to
>   keep vigilant and shout out 'Where are the
>   Terrorats?' And then *we'll* tell you. If we all
>   keep watching for them we'll all be safe! It'll
>   be a real Patriot Act! So let's try ... Now you
>   shout --
> Audience: Where are the Terrorats?
> Dick: Behind you!

At this point the audience all turn around and try to spot
the Terrorats in their midst, but they can't because the
Terrorats are sneaky and don't play by the rules. So the
only way for the audience to stay safe is to trust the brave
leaders onstage and unquestioningly agree to every measure they promote in their War on Terrorats.

The Pinto ends with a spectacular song and dance
number in which Cheneyton and the others proceed up
the slopes of Washington Hill and build themselves a vast

mansion. All the while they're singing an extraordinary rendition of a medley of Dixie Chicks songs. And they all live Happily Ever After.

The End. (As Tony the Poodle barks on his way out).

Obviously none of this is true. For there to be a link between Pinter and panto would be absurd.

But at times Britain is an absurd place. And all the better for it.

A WMD

~ 101 ~

If someone bumps into you
what should you do?

Apologise.

So Just How British am I?

Now that you know the answers to the One Hundred and One Essential Questions of Britishness you'll probably be wondering just how British you really are.

To help you find out, there follow two revision tests for you to attempt.

Take your time, and if you get stuck on any particular question then move on to the next, before returning to the tricky one when you've finished the rest. (And if you really get into difficulties, the answers are given on the pages after the tests.)

And remember to write on only one side of the paper and to show your workings where necessary.

Good Luck!

Your time starts ... now.

REVISION TEST ONE

1 How many teaspoons of tea should you add for 'the pot'?

2 How should you complain about someone who jumps a queue?

3 To what is 'Politically Correct' often shortened?

4 What was the name of Arthur Balfour's uncle?

5 During the hokey-cokey when you've finished bending your knees and stretching your arms what should you shout?

6 What don't and do cows go?

7 What is the connection between Oscar Wilde's Ernest and Anya Hindmarsh?

8 How much does 1001 clean 'a big, big carpet' for?

9 According to the cover of *Life in the United Kingdom: A Journey to Citizenship* what is the Home Office building?

10 What curry features in a pop song?

11 Where was the Magna Carta signed?

12 How often does a boat sink in The Boat Race?

13 What did the New Labour Party used to be called?

14 What makes Marmite such a valued source of nutrients?

15 Should you report your neighbour for using a hosepipe during a hosepipe ban?

16 Are Cliff Richard and Keith Richards actually brothers?

17 What is Yarg?

18 On only what particular occasion, allegedly, do the supporters of Grimsby Town Football Club sing?

19 What should you shout to stop a dropped conker from being crushed under foot?

20 Where didn't Edwina Currie keep her eggs?

21 Why don't the people who run the London
    Underground just fill in the gap?

22 In what year did BB Print Digital produce the
    2002 calendar *Roundabouts of Redditch*?

23 What story of child beating and wife murder is a
    traditional children's entertainment?

24 What is a WFI quotient?

25 Who's last words were 'I am just going outside
    and may be some time'?

26 Complete the following well know political
    soundbite: 'Education, Education............'

27 What time did the Chinaman go to the dentist?

28 For what is 'Norman Lamont' cockney rhyming
    slang?

29 Does the colour of the cliffs at Dover have
    anything to do with the bluebirds flying over
    them?

30 What is famously bigger on the inside than it is on
    the outside?

31 When the bowler is Holding who is the batsman?

32 Did more people vote for Neil Kinnock's party in the 1992 election when he lost by 22 seats than did for Tony Blair's party in the 2005 election when he won by 64 seats?

33 What fish best personifies Britain's favourite dance?

34 What was the name of the scientist in Thunderbirds?

35 Is there any connection between Bryan Haw and Lord Haw-Haw?

36 Would a trip to IKEA be quite so appealing without the prospect of a plate of the very reasonably priced Swedish meatballs as part of the deal?

37 What were the names of the two eighteenth-century coaching inns found in the Buckinghamshire town of Stony Stratford?

38 What was Chesney Hawkes one and only hit?

39 The 'wrong kind' of what stopped British Rail?

40 Have you tried turning it off and turning it on
    again?

REVISION TEST TWO

1 Of what tribe of ancient Britons was Boadicea the queen?

2 What part of a dog represents the highest form of praise?

3 Complete the first line of this stirring war movie theme tune: *Derr, der, der, derr, de-de, der...*

4 What is the '...great chieftain o' the pudding-race'?

5 Under what names did Ant & Dec have a hit with 'Let's Get Ready To Rhumble'?

6 You wait ages for a bus, then what happens?

7 Were the Krays or the Krankies more antisocial?

8 Whose effigy are children no longer encouraged to burn?

9 If the car park is full on a bank holiday at a beauty spot where should a Briton eat his sandwiches?

10 Why, why, why Delilah?

11 What was the name of the hamster that Freddie Starr didn't actually eat?

12 How many Oscars did Gandhi win?

13 What was Eddie 'The Eagle' Edwards' day job?

14 What kind of creature has been named after Sir David Attenborough?

15 Which traditional British family entertainment is, in many respects, a celebration of transvestisism?

16 What is the greatest-ever British newpaper sports headline?

17 What cut of meat was ennobled by King Henry the Eighth?

18 This Christmas who will a young George Michael still be giving his heart to?

19 Rhubarb is a popular British pudding ingredient. But who was Roobarb's cartoon partner?

20 Has Britain (and arguably the world) got more fraught since Michael Winner stopped appearing on TV saying 'Calm down, calm down'?

21 Name two modes of transport associated with gravy.

22 Why isn't Wales represented on the Union Jack?

23 Who was better, Jon Pertwee or Tom Baker?

24 Where does charity begin?

25 In the early part of Sir Elton John's career 'sorry' seemed to be the hardest word. What is it now?

26 How many mickles make a muckle?

27 Whose disfigured face featured on the cover of the Trex Pistols *God Save The Greens*?

28 How many holes does it take to fill the Albert Hall?

29 What was the name of Julian's friend?

30 What word links fox hunting with vegetarianism?

31 How did CJ get to where he was 'today'?

32 What's a Bath Oliver?

33 Where did 'Home improvement expert Harold Hill' live in the 1979 Ian Dury song 'This Is What We Find'?

34 Name the two most culturally significant dresses of the last thirty years.

35 What is the key ingredient of Laver bread?

36 How much does a peerage cost?

37 What three popular television programmes have been inspired by the depiction of the soul-destroying, totalitarian fascist state in George Orwell's *1984*?

38 Who are the only two people who've had to resign as a result of the war in Iraq?

39 Alan Bennett is a National Treasure. But in the event of fire, theft or damage is the cost of replacing him covered by our National Insurance payments?

40 Salt and vinegar?

Revision Test Answers

TEST ONE

1 One. 2 Under your breath. 3 Guardian reader. 4 Bob. (Robert Gascoyne Cecil). 5 Rah!Rah!Rah! 6 They don't go 'who', they do go 'moo'. 7 A handbag! 8 Less than half a crown. 9 A safe, just and tolerant society. 10 Korma in Culture Club's 'Korma Chameleon'. 11 Runnymede. 12 Not often enough. 13 Unelectable. 14 Vitamins. 15 It depends what he's doing with it. 16 No. 17 A cheese from Cornwall. 18 When they're fishing. 19 No stamps. 20 In her mouth. That was already filled with her foot. 21 Laziness. 22 2001. 23 Punch and Judy. 24 The Won't Fall In quotient of a dunked biscuit. 25 Captain Lawrence Edward Grace Oates. Somewhere near to the South Pole. On his 32nd birthday. 26 Top-up fees. 27 Tooth-hurtee. 28 Futon. 29 Quite possibly. 30 The Tardis. 31 Willey. 32 Yes. 1,997,387 more. 33 The conga eel. 34 Brains. 35 No. 36 No. 37 The Cock and The Bull. 38 'The One And Only'. 39 State subsidy. 40 Yes.

TEST TWO

1 The Iceni. 2 His bollocks. 3 *der*. 4 The haggis. 5 PJ and Duncan. 6 Three turn up. 7 The Krankies because The Krays 'only hurt their own'. 8 Guy Fawkes. 9 In the nearest lay-by. 10 No one really knows because before she

had the chance to explain herself she 'laughed no more' i.e. was murdered. 11 Supersonic. 12 Gandhi didn't win any. The movie *Gandhi* won eight. 13 Plasterer. 14 An echidna. 15 Panto. 16 'Super Cally Go Ballistic Celtic Are Atrocious'. 17 A loin of beef. 18 Someone special. 19 Custard. 20 Yes. 21 Boats and trains. 22 Because at the time the flag was created Wales was considered part of England and so already represented by the cross of St George. 23 Tom Baker. 24 At home. 25 It's not a word, but a phrase. ' Hey, d'you know what would be really nice ... one bunch of flowers!' 26 Many. 27 Mrs Beeton. 28 One. If it's big enough. 29 Sandy. 30 Quorn. 31 He never specified how he got to where he was 'today'. He only spelled out how he didn't get to where he was 'today'. 32 It's something you wash your body in, but my name's not Oliver. 33 Harold Hill. 34 Liz Hurley's Versace safety pin dress and Ginger Spice's Union Jack mini dress. 35 Lavers. 36 This is a trick question. Peerages are *not* for sale in Britain. 37 *Big Brother. Room 101. Trinny and Susannah Undress.* 38 Piers Morgan and Greg Dyke. 39 No. 40 Every time.

Grades

0–20 questions answered correctly.
Congratulations you've passed! You have achieved an A Grade.

21–40 questions answered correctly.
Congratulations you've passed! You have achieved an A* Grade.

41–60 questions answered correctly.
Congratulations you've passed! You have achieved an A** Grade.

61–79 questions answered correctly.
Congratulations you've passed! You have achieved an A** Version 2.0 Grade.

80 questions answered correctly.
*Congratulations you've passed! And you've achieved the highest, most coveted, rarest grade of all. You have achieved a **Fail**. Well done you!*

For all of you who have passed these revision exams an Official Certificate of Britishness can be downloaded from www.rbooks.co.uk/rulesbritannia. Once you have downloaded the certificate and filled in your name and grade you will need to get it verified and signed by a respected community figure like a GP, a magistrate, or an ex-member of The Sugababes.

If you have been affected by any of the issues raised in this book then make sure to buy copies for your friends so that they can be affected too. After all why should you suffer alone?